Wrigley Field: The Centennial

100 YEARS AT THE FRIENDLY CONFINES

Les Krantz

TRIUMPH
BOOKS

Contributing writers: Bill Chastain, Eric Short, Matthew Silverman, Marty Strasen, Sue Sveum
Video editor: Jack Piantino

Library of Congress Cataloging-in-Publication Data
Krantz, Les.
  Wrigley Field : the centennial : 100 years at the friendly confines / Les Krantz.
    pages cm
  Includes bibliographical references.
  ISBN 978-1-60078-834-5 (hardback)
1. Wrigley Field (Chicago, Ill.)—History. 2. Chicago Cubs (Baseball team)—History. I. Title.
  GV417.W75K73 2013
  796.357'640977311 2 23
                            2013023563

This book is available in quantity at special discounts for your group or organization. For further information, contact:
Triumph Books LLC
814 North Franklin
Chicago, Illinois 60610
(312) 337-0747
www.triumphbooks.com

Printed in China
ISBN: 978-1-60078-834-5
Design by Eileen Wagner Design

To my favorite companions at Wrigley Field, Ryan and Isabel ("Issy") Krantz: May the breezes from the ballpark as well as the winds of your time reward you—and the Cubbies too—with abundance of home runs!

Contents

Part IV: The Postwar Years Through the 1970s

Part V: 1980s and 1990s

Part VI: Modern Times (2000–2013)

Wrigley Field: The Centennial

100 YEARS AT THE FRIENDLY CONFINES

PART I

Building a Ballpark:
THE HISTORY OF WRIGLEY FIELD

Wrigley Field. Just the name evokes the image of warm, sunny days spent at the ballpark, the breeze blowing in off Lake Michigan. Or maybe it's blowing out, carrying home-run balls out onto Waveland Avenue. These are the Friendly Confines—home of the beloved Chicago Cubs.

The Chicago Whales emblem.

THE SECOND-OLDEST ballpark in the nation, Wrigley Field epitomizes America's pastime. At Wrigley, it's baseball the way baseball used to be. Babe Ruth played there. So did Lou Gehrig and Ted Williams. Ernie Banks, Ron Santo, and Sammy Sosa called Wrigley Field home. Wrigley Field is truly an icon.

But it wasn't always that way. Would the mystique remain if this were Weeghman Park? Who can even spell that? Who'd want to name their dog after *that* stadium? And would we want to root for the Chicago Federals (or Chi-Feds, as they were sometimes called)? Or the Whales? Because those are the teams that played at Weeghman.

Maybe we should back up a bit. At the start of the 20th century, Clark and Addison Streets, where Wrigley Field proudly stands today, were smack dab in the middle of a working-class neighborhood. The houses held two or three apartments each, mostly filled with factory workers and their families. The rest of the neighborhood was made up of factories and warehouses.

While the National League's Chicago Cubs were busy winning their first and only back-to-back World Series, in 1907 and 1908, at their home field, the West Side Club, the working stiffs who resided near Clark and Addison represented the nation's industry, *not* the national pastime.

The Friendly Confines.

Charlie Weeghman (left) and two associates at the Weeghman Park groundbreaking ceremony on March 4, 1914.

And then along came Charles Henry "Lucky Charlie" Weeghman. He was a prosperous businessman who earned his money the old-fashioned way—by working for it—and he found himself with a little extra cash around the same time the Federal League was trying to establish itself in baseball. Weeghman bought the Chicago Federals in 1914 and decided they needed a suitable place to play their games.

When a vacant North Side lot caught Weeghman's attention, he promptly leased the land and hired Zachery Taylor Davis, a well-known local architect, to design the future ballpark. Davis was already established in the Chicago baseball community; he had designed Comiskey Park for the major league White Sox just four years earlier. But Weeghman's field was never intended to compete with "the world's greatest baseball palace" on the South Side. Instead he created a ballpark that was the perfect size for the untested Federals and their fans. And it came in at half the price of Comiskey Park—a mere $250,000.

Construction of the 14,000-seat ballpark kicked off with a groundbreaking ceremony on March 4, 1914, and ended on April 23 of the same year with a parade, rose presentation, and—just like at baseball games today—the ceremonial throwing of the first pitch. With extra "circus seats" brought in for that first game, more than 21,000 baseball fans were on hand to watch the Chi-Feds beat Kansas City by a score of 9–1.

Weeghman was a baseball lover, but he soon learned that even with a winning season, owning a team in the Federal League was not the best investment. He was reluctant to put more money into making improvements at the park, but after a record number of home runs were hit over the left-field wall during that inaugural season, Weeghman agreed to have the left-field fence moved back 25 feet. The only other changes he made were to remove the right-field stands and double the left-field bleachers.

In 1915 the Chi-Feds were renamed the Whales—the result of a fan "naming contest." The team won the Federal League pennant that year and managed to keep those bleacher seats full. And when the Federal League disbanded that same year, Weeghman was in a position to buy himself a new National League baseball team: the Chicago Cubs.

Formerly a West Side team, the Cubs were owned at the time by Charles P. Taft (brother of former US President William Taft) and run by Charles H. Thomas, who both resided in Cincinnati. Finding it difficult to manage the team from afar, they agreed to sell 90 percent of the franchise to Weeghman and a few investors (including William Wrigley Jr.) for $500,000.

Merging the Whales with the Cubs on his first National League roster, Weeghman secured Joe Tinker (of Tinker-to-Evers-to-Chance fame) as manager and moved the team to his own Weeghman Park. In 1916 the Cubs officially became North Siders, playing at what is today the oldest National League ballpark. The Cubs defeated the Cincinnati Reds by a score of 7–6 in their debut game at the corner of Clark and Addison.

Weeghman really catered to his audience. He was the first owner to allow fans to keep foul balls and the first to set up food booths behind the stands. A popular guy? No doubt.

Financial difficulties, however, caused Weeghman to sell his interest to William Wrigley Jr. in 1918, and he renamed the ballpark Cubs Park in 1920. It wasn't until several years later that the chewing-gum magnate apparently had a revelation: what's the point of owning a baseball team if you can't name the park after yourself? In 1926 Wrigley Field was born. Along with the new name, the park got an upgrade that year when an upper deck was added to the grandstands, doubling the seating capacity.

For those fans who couldn't make it out to the ballpark, Wrigley turned to the airwaves to broadcast games throughout the Midwest starting in 1925. Critics feared this might keep fans *away* from the ballpark, but exactly the opposite came to pass. WGN Radio brought baseball into American homes, creating Cubs fans young and old, near and far—fans who

An ad for the Federal League's Opening Day, featuring the Chicago Whales at Weeghman Park.

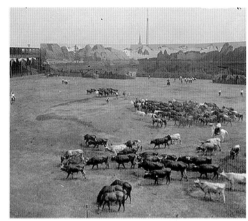

Buffalo Bill's Wild West Show prepares for a 1916 performance at West Side Park in Chicago.

Opening Day in 1914 at Weeghman Park.

The Chicago Federals on the field at Weeghman Park in 1914.

couldn't *wait* to attend a baseball game at storied Wrigley Field. In fact, in 1927 the Cubs became the first National League team to draw more than one million fans in a single season.

Today Wrigley Field is widely known for the ivy covering its outfield walls. Many a baseball has been lost amidst those vines over the years. In 1927 Bill Veeck, a 13-year-old popcorn vendor and son of then–Cubs president William Veeck Sr., came up with the idea of planting the ivy. He finally saw the idea become reality 10 years later when 350 bittersweet vines and 200 Boston ivy plants were put in. The Boston ivy eventually won out, and that's what covers the wall today.

Right behind those ivy-covered walls, you'll find the "Bleacher Bums" sitting in stands erected in 1937 to further increase the seating capacity at Wrigley Field. The manually operated 27-foot-high scoreboard that still stands today was also added at that time. And anyone passing by Wrigley Field after a game—both then and now—knows immediately how the Cubs fared. They need only look up to see which flag is flying atop the scoreboard—the white flag with a blue *W* practically shouts "Cubs Win!" while the blue flag with a white *L* reminds Cubs fans that there's always tomorrow.

Win or lose, the Cubs continued to draw fans, and June 27, 1930, marked the

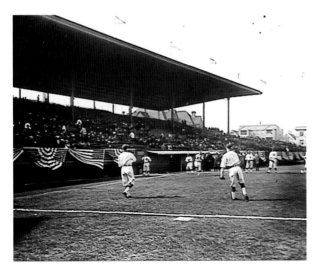

The Chicago Whales (formerly the Federals) on the field at Weeghman Park in 1914.

In 1914 Weeghman Park (now Wrigley Field) only had single-deck seating.

The 1914 Chi-Feds.

An exterior shot of Weeghman Park in 1914.

Chicago Mayor William Hale Thompson throws out the first pitch at Weeghman Park before the start of the 1915 Chicago Whales season.

largest crowd ever—51,556. Unfortunately it was a Ladies' Day promotion that day, so only 19,748 were paying guests. On hand to watch the Cubs play the Dodgers, the crowd hoped to see outfielder Hack Wilson club one of his 56 homers. It didn't happen, but in September of that year, Wilson collected his 190th and 191st RBIs—a number that still stands as a major league record.

The 1930s saw at least two other memorable moments in baseball. The first was hardly a fan favorite. It was in October 1932, the third game of the World Series, when Babe Ruth supposedly gestured to the outfield, predicting the home run he was about to hit. Witnesses gave different accounts, and it was never verified, but the Yankee slugger's "called shot" remains part of baseball lore to this day.

The second, in 1938, was Gabby Hartnett's home run in the ninth inning of a tie game. His winning shot became known as the "Homer in the Gloamin" when the outfielder hit the ball out of the park and into the darkening evening to catapult the Cubs into first place. It's too bad there was no organ on hand back then to celebrate the moment. Wrigley Field later set the tone—and the trend—in 1941 for organs, which became standard equipment at ballparks across the nation.

And who can forget 1945? That's the year that all Cubs fans have

The 1915 Chicago Whales.

emblazoned on their hearts, marking the last time the Cubs made it to the World Series. The Cubbies put up a valiant effort, winning three postseason games, but lost out to the Tigers, who won four.

Other highlights of the decade include Wrigley's largest paid attendance ever. A record-setting crowd of 46,572 was on hand to witness Jackie Robinson's Chicago debut in May 1947. And then there was WGN-TV's premiere broadcast in 1948 with Jack Brickhouse at the helm.

The 1950s were a disappointment to the Wrigley Field fans; the park sat empty during the postseason for the entire decade. (Well, actually for the next four and a half decades, but who's counting?) On the bright side, newcomer Ernie Banks hit his first major league home run in 1953 and later became the first National League player to win the MVP trophy in back-to-back seasons (1948 and '49). And

Two shots of Mordecai Brown with the Chicago Cubs: left, in 1909 at West Side Park; right, in 1916 at Weeghman Park.

in an unlikely—and unlucky—moment in time, June 30, 1959, became known for the infamous "two balls in play" game. A wild pitch sent Cardinal Stan Musial to first base, but havoc ensued when he attempted to steal an extra base. Third baseman Alvin Dark had the original ball (recovered from the wild pitch), while pitcher Bob Anderson held a new ball issued by the umpire. Both Cubs fired to the unsuspecting second baseman—at the same time. St. Louis won.

In 1960 P.K. Wrigley came up with the—in hindsight—terrible idea of

A pensive Weeghman considers the fate of his team…and his park.

A panoramic of the crowd at the renamed Cubs Park in July 1929.

William Wrigley Jr. came to Chicago in 1891 with $32. Not long after, he owned an empire.

In 1920 a 17-year-old Lou Gehrig (pictured) and his NYC Commerce High baseball team came to the newly renamed Cubs Park to play Lane Tech in what was billed as a "High School Championship" game. The young Gehrig hit a dinger that cleared the bleachers in right and went across the street outside the park.

Sweet Home Chicago.

Bill Veeck Jr. (right) and an unknown man plant the iconic ivy along Wrigley Field's walls in 1937.

instigating a College of Coaches in place of a traditional manager. Five years later, the idea was chucked, and Leo Durocher took over as the Cubs skipper. Cubs fans will also remember the excitement of 1969, when Billy Williams, Ron Santo, and Ferguson Jenkins led the Cubs to a 92-win season. Unfortunately, a late run by the Mets won New York the pennant—along with the undying and everlasting resentment of Cubs fans everywhere.

By the 1980s Wrigley Field was widely known for its storied traditions—and for being home to baseball's

One of the many surrounding rooftops where people gather to watch the games at Wrigley Field.

These lights were not added at Wrigley Field until 1988, ushering in the night game at the Friendly Confines.

loveable losers. The Tribune Company bought the Friendly Confines from the Wrigleys in 1981 for $20.5 million. Later in the decade, there was much debate over adding lights to Wrigley Field, with forward-thinking proponents encouraging the ballclub to keep pace with the other more high-tech teams and the purists wanting to maintain the traditions of this historical gem. Wrigley Field finally did add lights—and night games—in 1988. But what a lot of people—even the staunchest of Cubs fans—may not know is that lights were actually *scheduled* to be installed as early as 1942. The bombing of Pearl Harbor and the US entry into World War II caused Phil Wrigley to instead donate those lights to the government for the war effort.

Other bright spots in the 1980s were the debut of Ryne Sandberg in 1982 and a National League East title in 1989 to cap the exciting decade.

Rookie pitcher Kerry Wood tied a major league record in 1998 when he struck out 20 batters, and in 1999 Sammy Sosa became the first major leaguer to hit 60 homers in back-to-back seasons. Wrigley renovations included the addition of 63 private boxes and the old ballpark's first-ever elevator. The Cubs even clinched a wild-card berth in 1998 but failed to advance. But even sadder in 1998 were the deaths of Cubs broadcasters Harry Caray and Jack Brickhouse. The seventh-inning stretch would never be the same again at Wrigley Field without a bespectacled Caray leading the fans in his enthusiastic rendition of "Take Me Out to the Ballgame."

The 21st century brought a series of highs and lows for the Cubs at Wrigley Field. But win or lose, Cubs fans stayed loyal. In 2005 the fans saw an expansion of the bleachers and the addition of a restaurant that overlooks the field. A Wrigley Field attendance record of 3,303,200 was set in 2008—almost 600,000 more than the National League average.

And for those who can't get a ticket to Wrigley—or prefer not to—there are always the Wrigley rooftops. The flat-roofed apartment buildings behind the outfield have been there as long as Wrigley Field itself. Unlike some other big-league ballparks that go out of their way to *block* the view for nonpaying fans, Wrigley Field embraced the concept. What started as a few apartment-dwellers having a barbeque has expanded to include bleacher seats, open bars, and lots of food. The building owners have agreed to split the profits with the Cubs organization, and those apartment seats are now considered Wrigley Field Part 2—almost like having a seat in the upper (and over) deck.

One can only imagine the look of surprise on the faces of 1914 Chicagoans if they could see the ballpark today. While many of the buildings still stand, the area's demographic has changed drastically. Factory workers have given way to young professionals who can easily hop the "L" or ride a bus to their jobs in the Loop. Part of the Lakeview neighborhood, this is Wrigleyville. Bordered by Ashland Avenue and Roscoe Street, Byron and Halstead Streets, this thriving neighborhood is home to a wealth of restaurants and bars. And if most of them cater to the Cubs fans who frequent the area, well…that's okay.

When the Tribune Company sold the Cubs to the Ricketts family in 2009 for a whopping $845 million, Tom Ricketts knew better than to promise the fans a World Series championship—or even a World Series berth. But hope is still alive at Wrigley Field, and it always will be. The Friendly Confines beckon to baseball fans year in and year out. Whether the team is winning or losing, Wrigley Field will always be home. Here, it's *always* "a beautiful day for a ballgame."

The Early Years (1918–1929)

The late 1910s and 1920s saw some major changes at Wrigley, including the arrival of the Cubs in 1916 and two name changes (to Cubs Park in 1920 and finally Wrigley Field in 1926). Despite winning the NL pennant in 1918 and 1929, the Cubs just couldn't get it done on the big stage, losing the 1929 World Series to the Philadelphia Athletics.

Ticket stub from the 1918 World Series, Game 3.

1918: FIRST PLACE JUST WASN'T GOOD ENOUGH

*L*OOKING AHEAD TO the 1918 season, Charles Weeghman hoped to bolster the Cubs roster to where the finished product could claim the National League pennant. The Cubs president didn't land the player he targeted, but he did manage to put together a quality club capable of living up to his high standards.

Weeghman tried to pry talented second baseman Rogers Hornsby away from the Cardinals, offering them two quality players and $50,000. Alas, the Cardinals didn't bite on the deal that would have sent "the Rajah" to Chicago, so Weeghman shifted gears and focused on finding pitching to complement his 23-game winner Hippo Vaughn.

First the team acquired Grover Cleveland Alexander and another player from the Phillies in exchange for two players and a reported $55,000. Alexander had gone 30–13 the previous season. Next Weeghman acquired Lefty Tyler—who had won 14 games and posted a 2.52 ERA for the Braves in 1917—for two players and $15,000. The acquisitions set the tone for the team the Cubs put on the field in 1918—one that could pitch, field, and had uncommonly good timing at the plate. In

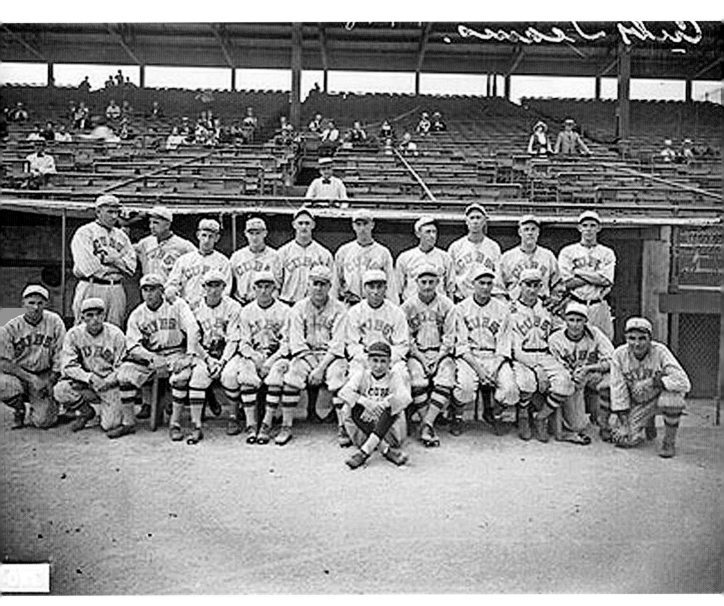

The 1918 Chicago Cubs.

Chicago Cubs 1918 5¢ Official Score Card from the now-defunct soft drink Bevo.

addition, they were able to overcome adversity, like when they lost Alexander to the army at the end of April. Nevertheless, the team continued to roll, a fact epitomized by a come-from-behind 9–8 win over the Reds at Weeghman Park when they scored four in the ninth. When the Cubs beat the Phillies 3–0 in Philadelphia on June 6, they took over first place. They did not relinquish the position for the remainder of the season, which was shortened to 140 games due to World War I.

Vaughn's brilliance on the mound could be seen time and again throughout the season. The left-hander kicked off the season at Weeghman Park with a 2–0 complete-game one-hitter over the Cardinals. And on July 6 he did everything in a 1–0 win over the Giants, again at Weeghman Park. Not only did he go the distance in the 12-inning affair, he also singled home the winning run.

The Cubs clinched the pennant with a doubleheader sweep over the Reds at Weeghman Park on August 20. Tyler tossed a complete-game gem in a 1–0 win in the first game. Claude Hendrix won his 20th game of the season in the Cubs' 6–4 win in the second game.

The club finished with a record of 84–45 to win the pennant by 10½ games. The team ranked first in ERA at 2.18, well under the 2.76 National League average, and they allowed the fewest runs in the league, 393, while leading the league in runs scored with 538. Shortstop Charlie Hollocher led the team in batting average (.316), on-base percentage (.379), slugging percentage (.397), and stolen bases (26). Vaughn led the team in wins (22), strikeouts (148), and ERA (1.74).

By winning the National League pennant, the Cubs earned the right to meet the Boston Red Sox in the World Series, which began on September 5, 1918.

Boston had not lost a World Series in four previous trips. To the 1918 Fall Classic they brought a dominating pitching staff that included Joe Bush, Carl Mays, and Sam Jones. In addition the Red Sox had a secret weapon in Babe Ruth, a young man who had broken into the major leagues as a pitcher but in 1918 began to split time between the mound and the outfield, with astonishing results. Ruth led the

Before a 1918 World Series game, Weeghman (left) stands with Cubs manager Fred Mitchell.

Four Chicago Cubs prepare before a World Series game in 1918.

Babe Ruth (seen here during the 1918 World Series) became known for being a slugger, but he was also one of the best pitchers of his era.

American League with 11 home runs, and he hit .300 while compiling 13 wins.

Oddly, the first game of the World Series was played at Comiskey Park, due to the larger seating capacity at the White Sox's home park. Facing a hostile crowd, Ruth shut down the Cubs in Game 1 by pitching a complete game in a 1–0 Red Sox win. The only run of the game came when Stuffy McInnis singled to left off Vaughn to drive home Dave Shean.

Tyler pitched the Cubs to a 3–1 win in Game 2, also played at Comiskey Park. Tyler even helped himself with a two-run single in the three-run second inning. The game also featured a brawl between Red Sox third-base coach Charley Wagner and Cubs coach Otto Knabe in the top of the third inning. Wagner's verbal

Dode Paskert practices before a 1918 World Series game.

Max Flack in the dugout during the 1918 World Series.

harassment of Tyler instigated the fight. Defending Tyler, Knabe invited Wagner into the Cubs dugout to settle the matter. Wagner went into the dugout, but he didn't fare so well. According to the *New York Times*, Knabe "brushed up the floor of the dugout with Wagner."

The World Series remained in Chicago—and Comiskey Park—for Game 3, on September 7. Vaughn had gone the distance in the opening game of the Series, and he started Game 3 after a day's rest, which did not pay off. The Red Sox scored twice in the fourth on singles by Wally Schang and Everett Scott, and they were the only runs needed in a 2–1 win.

When the Series moved to Boston's Fenway Park for Game 4, a well-rested Ruth made his second start and extended his postseason scoreless streak to 29 consecutive innings before the Cubs snapped the streak with two runs in the eighth. But two runs weren't enough as the Red Sox took a 3–2 win. Ruth also led Boston's offense with a two-run triple in the fourth inning.

Vaughn rebounded to deliver in Game 5 when he spun a five-hit shutout in a 3–0 win to cut the Red Sox's Series lead to 3–2.

The teams almost did not play Game 6 due to the players' displeasure about the reduced revenue from gate receipts. (For the first time, all first-division clubs received a portion of the revenue.) Once the matter was resolved, the Cubs' hopes of winning the final two games disappeared in a 2–1 loss that ended the Series.

It would seem that the parents of GROVER CLEVELAND ALEXANDER, having given him such a name, had political aspirations for their infant boy. Little did they know that "Pete" Alexander would grow up to be one of the best baseball players of his era and one of the greatest Cubs of all time.

Born in 1887, the future pitcher chose baseball over law and began his career in 1909 in Galesburg, of the Illinois-Missouri League. His first season was pretty remarkable—three shutouts, a 1.36 batting average, and a blow to the temple on a double-play throw. He was unconscious for two and a half days. As a result of the accident, he experienced double vision for nine months before it simply disappeared.

The Philadelphia Phillies drafted him in 1911 for a whopping $500. They got their money's worth when Alexander pitched a league-leading 31 complete games, struck out 227 batters, and ended the season with a 28–13 record. The Cubs acquired the 6'1" right-hander in 1917. Unfortunately, this transaction became known as one of the worst Cubs deals of all time when Alexander was drafted in 1918.

World War I took its toll on Alexander. He drank heavily and suffered from epilepsy and PTSD. He did win a Triple Crown in 1920, posting a 1.72 ERA, which is still the lowest for any Cubs pitcher at Wrigley Field. But his drinking forced the Cubs to trade him to the Cardinals in 1926.

Alexander was elected to the National Baseball Hall of Fame in 1938 and died in 1950 at age 63.

PETE ALEXANDER (1918–1926)

A swing and a…hit! Gehrig blasts it out of the park.

1920: GEHRIG'S EPIC PREP SCHOOL BLAST

ON JUNE 18, 1920—the day before he turned 17—Lou Gehrig played for New York City's Commerce High and doubled twice to lead a 6–5 win over Brooklyn's Commercial High in the New York City Championship Game. The spoils came in a trip to Chicago to play Lane Tech High in what would be billed as a "High School Championship" game between the two metropolitan high school powers.

For Gehrig, leading his team to victory turned out to be a somewhat easier task than actually getting to Chicago for the game scheduled for June 26 at Cubs Park. Gehrig needed his parents' permission, and they didn't like him playing sports in the first place. If they'd had their way, Gehrig would have paid more attention to his studies so he could go to college and become an engineer. So Gehrig's mother's refusal to grant her permission came as no surprise. Rather, the surprise came when her normally subservient son would not take no for an answer. Only after Gehrig's coach assured his mother of her son's safety on the trip did Gehrig receive her permission.

Gehrig had always been sheltered by his parents, which made the trip even more intoxicating to him. Not only did he

What is it with baseball nicknames, anyway? The unassuming CHARLES LEO HARTNETT was born in 1900, but "Gabby" went on to baseball fame. He was a great catcher and a hitting threat, best known for his game-winning walk-off "Homer in the Gloamin," a home run belted into the dusk during the Cubs' 1938 pennant run.

Hartnett followed in his father's footsteps with a love of baseball and an extraordinarily strong throwing arm. In 1920 he was given a job—so he could play on the company baseball team. His first pro contract came in 1921 with the Worcester Boosters.

The Cubs signed the 6'1" right-hander in 1922 for $2,500. Painfully shy as a rookie, Hartnett's teammates called him Gabby. But his actions spoke louder than words, giving him the last laugh. When the Cubs' catcher was injured in 1923, Hartnett got the job and held it for 18 seasons; he was well known as an all-around great guy. With 16 homers and a solid .299 batting average, Hartnett came in 15th in voting for the National League MVP his first year.

In 1925 he broke the home-run record for catchers with 24 and followed that up with two more great seasons. In 1929 he suffered an arm "deadness" but came back in 1930 with a .339 batting average.

Hartnett's best season came in 1935, when he led the Cubs to the World Series. With just nine errors and a .344 batting average, he was voted National League MVP.

In 1955 Hartnett was elected to the National Baseball Hall of Fame, and he later died in 1972, at age 72.

GABBY HARTNETT
(1922–1940)

Ticket stub from the 1920 High School Championship game at Wrigley Field where a 17-year-old Lou Gehrig hit a homer out of the park and across the street.

get to travel by train to a new city, he was able to eat and sleep on the train, and once in Chicago, he got to stay in a hotel. An added experience came when Gehrig and his team shared their train with former President of the United States William Taft, who told the team he looked forward to watching them play.

Cubs Park hosted a crowd of 10,000 for the game, and spectators were treated to an exciting contest that saw Commerce take an 8–6 lead into the ninth inning. However, a two-run lead looked like a precarious buffer for Commerce—particularly on Lane Tech's home turf.

Gehrig stood a chiseled six feet tall and weighed 200 pounds, giving him an intimidating presence. Nevertheless, he had gone hitless in five at-bats when he stepped to the plate with the bases loaded at the top of the ninth. No doubt frustrated, Gehrig did not allow that frustration to affect his patience.

He took the first pitch for strike one. Lane Tech wasn't so lucky on their next offering. Gehrig swung at the second pitch and made solid contact, resulting in a drive that cleared the bleachers in right and went across the street outside Cubs Park.

Commerce won the game, but Gehrig's power had stolen the show.

An account in the *Chicago Tribune* said it all: "Gehrig's blow would have made any big leaguer proud, yet it was walloped by a boy who hasn't yet started to shave."

Pitcher Jimmy Ring.

1922: CUBS DEFEAT PHILLIES IN 49-RUN SLUGFEST

O N ANY GIVEN day during the lengthy baseball season, a game can turn into something memorable, even historic.

That's what happened when the Philadelphia Phillies showed up to play the Chicago Cubs on August 25, 1922, in the first game of a three-game series at Cubs Park.

A look at that day's standings showed two teams experiencing dramatically different seasons. Manager Bill Killefer's Cubs sat in third place in the National League with a record of 66–53, while Key "Kaiser" Wilhelm's Phillies were 40–71, seventh place in the eight-team league.

Tony Kaufmann started for the Cubs and held the Phillies scoreless in the first inning. His teammates then pushed one across in the bottom half of the frame against Phillies starter Jimmy Ring to put the Cubs up 1–0. The tone of the game changed in the second inning. The Phillies scored three, and the Cubs answered with 10. The Phillies chipped away at the lead by scoring two in the third. Ring even seemed to settle down a bit when he held the Cubs scoreless in the third. The Phillies added another run in the fourth to cut the Cubs' lead to five runs.

But when the Cubs batted in the fourth, the bottom fell out for the Phillies. Ring retired just one Cubs batter in the fourth and got the early hook from Wilhelm, who brought in Lefty Weinert. By the time Weinert got the final two outs of the inning, the Cubs had crossed the plate 14 times to take what appeared to be a commanding 25–6 lead.

Marty Callaghan actually batted three times in the inning, accruing two hits and striking out once in the process.

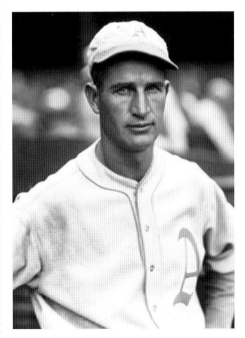

DeWitt LeBourveau.

Pitching was far from the Phillies' only problem in the fourth. While the Cubs scored 16 runs against Ring—who walked five in his three-and-a-third-inning stint—just six of the runs were earned.

Given the large deficit, Wilhelm opted to leave Weinert on the mound for the remainder of the game. In stark contrast to the texture of the game in the first four innings, the Phillies and Weinert held the Cubs to just one more run for the remainder of the game.

Meanwhile, the Phillies offense suddenly came to life, scoring three in the fifth and eight in the eighth. The visitors had already scored six times in the ninth against Earnest "Tiny" Osborne when DeWitt LeBourveau stepped to the plate with two outs and the bases loaded. But Osborne struck out LeBourveau to preserve the Cubs' 26–23 win.

Suffice to say, plenty of runs were scored amid the 51-hit, 23-walk, 10-error affair, but more runs potentially could have been scored given the fact that 25 runners were left on base. Still, the 49 runs remain the major league record for the most runs ever scored in a game.

Perhaps the most amazing statistic of the day is that both teams scored all those runs in just 3:01 of game time.

1929: DOMINATION TURNS TO DOOM

EVERYTHING FELL INTO place for the 1929 Cubs—from the management to the players to the fans—when the Cubs experienced one of the best seasons in franchise history. In the end, the only thing that didn't go their way was the weather.

Joe McCarthy managed the '29 Cubs, demonstrating an acumen that would lead him to the Hall of Fame before his managing career was complete. Plenty of times he made in-game choices that made the difference between winning and losing. But any decisions he made during games paled in comparison to the way he handled Hack Wilson.

Cubs slugger Wilson liked to imbibe during a period of American history in which Prohibition made drinking alcohol illegal. Drinkers followed Wilson's lead by taking their thirst to the barstools of speakeasies in the Windy City. Though Wilson drank too much on many occasions, McCarthy exercised prudence when disciplining his slugger, a proactive approach well ahead of its time. As a result, McCarthy got the best out of Wilson, who went on to hit .345 with 39 home runs and 159 RBIs in 1929.

Rogers Hornsby gets a single for the Cubbies in Game 3 of the 1929 Series.

Wilson was one of many sluggers in a Cubs lineup that included Charlie Grimm, Woody English, Riggs Stephenson, and Kiki Cuyler. In addition, the 1929 Cubs had a new face in Rogers Hornsby, who Cubs management had acquired in an off-season trade with the Boston Red Sox, for four players and $200,000. "The Rajah" proceeded to hit .380 with 39 home runs and 149 RBIs en route to earning National League Most Valuable Player honors.

After rolling through their National League schedule, the Cubs clinched the pennant on September 18, 1929. Despite losing 7–3 to the Giants that day, the loss did not matter, because the Pittsburgh Pirates lost the first game of a doubleheader with the Boston Braves that day. The Pirates' loss came minutes before the Cubs' loss had been minted, thereby sealing the pennant for the Cubs.

When the 5–4 Braves win was posted on the scoreboard at Wrigley Field,

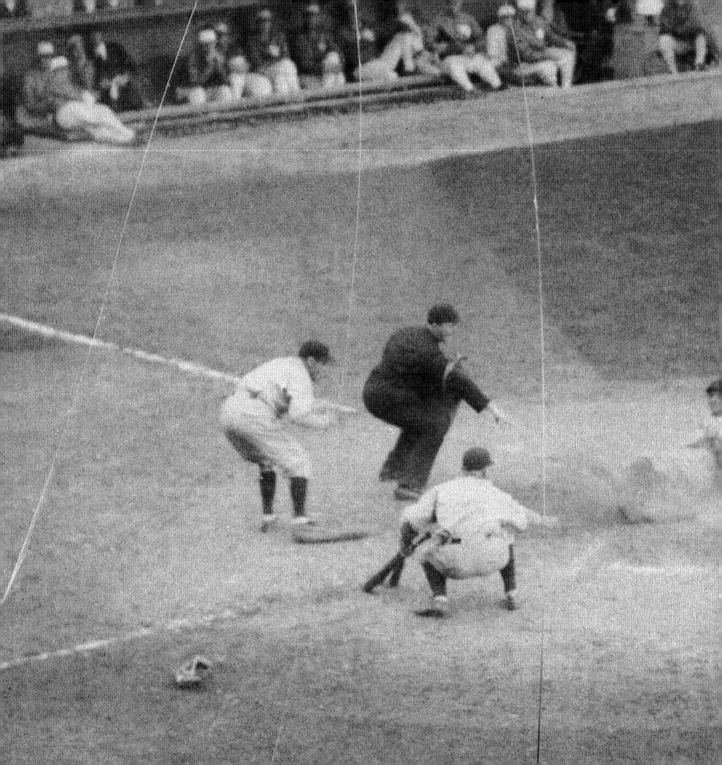

Cub Riggs Stephenson scores for Chicago in 1929 World Series action against the Athletics.

some in the crowd of 10,000 applauded. Others sat on their hands, obviously not understanding the significance of the win, which gave the Cubs their first pennant since 1918. The Cubs finished the season with a comfortable 10½-game lead, earning the team a spot in the World Series against the Philadelphia Athletics on October 8, 1929, and suggesting to their fans that a dynasty could be in the making.

Connie Mack managed the Athletics and opted to take a chance in Game 1 of the Fall Classic, in front of a crowd of 50,740 at Wrigley Field.

Charlie Root started for the Cubs, but the cagey Mack remained noncommittal about naming his starter for the opener. Most figured Mack would tap Grove, who had won 20 games that season, or George Earnshaw, who had won 24. Instead he went with veteran Howard Ehmke, who mixed speeds well but lacked any velocity on his fastball at that point in his career.

A minor disturbance occurred prior to the game when hot dog vendors inside Wrigley Field grew angry after finding out that a group of rogue vendors was selling hot dogs outside the gates, to the large crowd that had gathered hoping to buy bleacher tickets. Another oddity saw the game get delayed several minutes because the umpires showed up late.

Once the game began, Ehmke became the story. Cubs hitters were primed to feast on fastballs. Instead they were frustrated by a steady diet of Ehmke's soft stuff. While Ehmke moved effortlessly through the Cubs lineup, Jimmie Foxx homered off Root in the seventh to give the Athletics a 1–0 lead. In the ninth the Athletics scored twice to take a 3–0 lead. The Cubs managed to rally once in the ninth, but it wasn't enough, and they took a 3–1 loss. Ehmke went the distance, setting a World Series record by striking out 13.

In Game 2, Foxx hit a three-run homer and Al Simmons added a two-run blast to lead the Athletics to a 9–3 win.

Once again Cubs hitters struggled to make contact against the Athletics pitchers as Earnshaw and Grove struck out 13 in a combined effort. Only Wilson seemed to be locked in, as he had three hits in the game.

The Series moved to Shibe Park in Philadelphia for Game 3 on October 11. Guy Bush started for the Cubs and came through with a complete game, and his teammates scored three times in the sixth inning in a 3–1 win. Suddenly the Cubs trailed by just one game.

With confidence restored, the Cubs took an 8–0 lead in Game 4 with 29,921 watching at Shibe Park. When the Athletics batted in the eighth, only six outs stood between the Cubs tying the series at two games each. Miraculously, the Athletics rallied, scoring 10 runs in the eighth to take a 10–8 win.

Wilson wore goat horns for his part in the Athletics' comeback. Playing center field, with a brutal sun shining in his face, the stocky Wilson lost two balls in the sun, including Mule Haas' blast that turned into a three-run inside-the-park home run. The rally is the only time in World Series history that a team rallied to win after falling behind by eight or more runs.

Trailing 3–1 in the Series, the Cubs hoped to take Game 5 in Philadelphia. If they could somehow force a Game 6 and a Game 7 in front of their home fans at Wrigley Field, the Cubs felt that they could rally to claim the Series. But the Cubs faithful never had the opportunity to cheer on their beloved team. Chicago took a 3–2 loss in Game 5, ending a magical summer in disappointment.

Baseball fans packed the rooftops of row houses surrounding sold-out Shibe Park to watch the Cubs play the Athletics in a 1929 World Series game.

PART III

The Great Depression and World War II (1930–1945)

The economy was in the doldrums, but the Cubs were flying high, winning National League pennants in 1932, 1935, 1938, and 1945 but losing the World Series every time. But even today, fans are still crying, "Next year!"

1932: BABE'S CALLED SHOT

The news media had a special "Cubs badge" that allowed them entrance to Wrigley Field to cover the World Series against the Yankees in 1932.

AS THE GREAT Depression deepened across the country in 1932, baseball attendance sagged noticeably. Nevertheless, the emotions on the field were as strong as ever. A striking example occurred on the Fourth of July at Yankee Stadium, when gentlemanly catcher Bill Dickey broke the jaw of Washington's Carl Reynolds in a one-punch fight following a collision at home plate.

Dickey was one of the Yankees' few holdovers from the previous decade—and one of the key players who would lead the team to greater dominance in the 1930s. Babe Ruth was 37 and slowing, but Lou Gehrig was still productive, hitting .349 with 151 RBIs in 1932. On the hill, Lefty Gomez and Red Ruffing became an irrepressible 1-2 punch; they would carry the Yankees the rest of the decade.

In the 1932 World Series, the Yankees had plenty of motivation to beat the Chicago Cubs. New York manager Joe McCarthy had been unceremoniously fired by the team near the end of the 1930 season. Moreover, Cubs shortstop Mark Koenig, a former Yankees mainstay whom the Cubs had acquired midseason, was voted only a half-share of a World Series bonus, despite his brilliant play for Chicago. The Yankees rightfully felt that their old friend had been slighted. During the Series,

Babe Ruth backs up from the plate in anticipation of a walk.

It was bad news both at Wrigley Field and at the movies, too, where the nation saw this newsreel about the Cubs' demise in '32.

UNIVERSAL NEWSPAPER NEWSREEL

CHICAGO, ILL.—

YANKEES SLAUGHTER CUBS, 4 STRAIGHT, TO WIN WORLD'S SERIES

insults were exchanged between the dugouts. Fans at Wrigley Field directed their hostilities at Ruth, the most vocal of the Yankees.

The '32 Yankees were full of swagger. They were making their first World Series appearance since 1928, but they had won that year and the year before in four-game sweeps. The Chicago Cubs had turned their season around late, largely because of the .353 batting of new teammate Mark Koenig. But the tightfisted Cubs voted Koenig only a one-half World Series share. The Yanks made the Cubs pay

in another way, throttling them on the field in Games 1 and 2 in New York.

For Game 3, Wrigley Field in Chicago was roaring from the benches to the outfield seats. Everybody was screaming at everybody. The score was tied at 4–4 when Ruth came to bat to face Charlie Root. Strike one. The Babe saucily held up one finger. After two balls and another strike, the Babe proved again that he knew the count. The Cubs were going bonkers at his audacity, spewing more verbal abuse, calling Ruth fat and old.

Ruth was waving his bat around, pointing it toward the Cubs dugout. A film discovered in 1992 seems to indicate that he pointed it toward the outfield. Some players and fans insisted that Ruth was calling his shot, while others claimed he was motioning toward the Chicago bench. Root was saying things unsuitable for delicate ears. Ruth replied by sending the next pitch into deep center, the longest home run at Wrigley Field that anyone could remember.

What is indisputable is that Ruth deposited pitcher Charlie Root's next pitch into the center-field bleachers, a towering blast that took the life out of the Cubs. Ruth's homer—forever known as the "called shot"—was followed by a Gehrig home run and an eventual 7–5 Yankees victory. Ruth snickered as he rounded the bases and basked in all the attention.

The called shot was indeed a Ruthian moment, one of the most indelible in World Series history. And it overshadowed the Yankees' third World Series sweep, as Ruth's team manhandled the Cubs with 37 runs in the four games. In fact, the Cubs posted a team ERA of 9.26, which remains the highest in World Series history. For Burleigh Grimes (23.63 ERA) and his fellow moundsmen, it was a Series to forget.

One historian called it "one of the largest legends of all time for the largest legend of all time." What Babe Ruth did— or didn't do—in the top of the fifth inning

When the Cubs came home for Game 3 of the 1932 World Series, the Loop—Chicago's downtown business district—was packed with revelers as the team paraded through the confetti before the game.

Team owner William Veeck Sr. helps a secretary wade through the barrage of ticket requests for the 1932 World Series.

Yankees immortal Lou Gehrig shakes Babe Ruth's hand as he crosses home plate after a World Series homer in '32, believed to be the Babe's legendary "called shot."

The Cubs autographed this ball—and surprisingly neatly too, considering it was with the old ink pens before ballpoints were common.

of Game 3 of the 1932 World Series is still debated by baseball historians.

For years afterward, the Babe would relish telling the story of how he had announced his home run. He told an interviewer, "That's the first time I ever got the players and the fans going at the same time. I never had so much fun in my whole life."

Root's story was different. "If he had tried that," he said, "the next pitch would have been in his ear."

HACK WILSON was larger than life. While not a tall man, the Cubs' acclaimed center fielder weighed in at 195 pounds. He was built like a beer keg on a 5'6" frame. And between his baseball accomplishments and his off-the-field antics, he was a well-known and beloved figure in Chicago.

Born in Pennsylvania in 1900, Lewis Robert Wilson was dubbed "Hack" due to his resemblance to a popular Russian wrestler who shared the same build. He boasted a size 18 collar but only a size 6 shoe. But as opposing pitchers soon discovered, he was all muscle.

The Cubs acquired Wilson after the Giants sent him to the minors. In an apparent clerical error, the Giants never renewed their option—and the Cubs picked him up at the bargain price of $5,000.

In 1925 Wilson hit an unremarkable .239, but sporting a Cubs uniform the next year, Wilson began a streak of five consecutive .300+ seasons with the Cubs. He got better every year, with 1930 one for the record books. That season, Wilson had a batting average of .356, hit 56 homers (a record that lasted 68 years), drove in 191 runs (a record that still stands today), and was elected National League MVP.

In his last year with the Cubs, his batting average dropped to .261. He died in 1948 and was elected to the National Baseball Hall of Fame in 1979.

Hack Wilson, on March 29, 1930.

HACK WILSON
(1926–1931)

1935: SIZZLING STREAK PRODUCES 100 WINS, WORLD SERIES BERTH

THE CUBS HAD more than a case of the "Monday blues" after dropping the second game of a doubleheader, 4–2, against the Cincinnati Reds on September 2, 1935, at Wrigley Field. They finished the day in third place in the National League standings, behind the "Whiz Kid" Cardinals and second-place Mets. Chicago's 79–52 record was nothing to sneeze at, certainly, but there was little evidence to suggest the North Siders were on the verge of a record-setting run to the pennant.

After a day off, the Cubs began a four-game sweep of the Phillies that included back-to-back 3–2 extra-inning wins at Wrigley. Another four-game home stand produced four victories over the lowly Braves. The Dodgers were next into the visitors' clubhouse, and Chicago erupted for 41 runs in a four-game sweep that vaulted the Cubs into first place for the first time since Opening Day.

Before they lost another game—on September 28, the penultimate day of the season—the Cubs had soared to a franchise record–tying 21-game winning streak. The first 18 of those victories came

Cubs team owner and chewing-gum magnate Philip K. Wrigley.

at the Friendly Confines, where their 56–21 record was the best home mark in the majors. They posted 100 wins for the first time in a quarter-century to earn a World Series date with the American League–champion Detroit Tigers.

The Cubs did it in unorthodox fashion. Pitcher Lon Warneke, in fact, called the summer of 1935 "the funniest baseball season I ever spent." The season was less than two weeks old when Cubs shortstop Billy Jurges and Pirates base runner Cookie Lavagetto traded punches in the infield after Lavagetto made a hard slide

An argument started during this World Series Game when the Cubs protested umpire George Moriarty's decision that Phil Cavarretta was out at second on an attempted steal.

Yes, Chicago was proud of the Cubs winning the National League championship, but they ultimately lost the '35 Series to the Detroit Tigers.

Cubs players celebrate after winning the National League pennant in 1935.

into second base during an April 29 game at Wrigley. A dugout-clearing brawl followed, after which the Cubs pushed home 10 runs in the eighth inning to emerge with a 12–11 victory.

The drama of a crazy season was long forgotten, however, by the time Charlie Grimm's Cubs prepared to battle the Tigers for the World Series crown. Detroit auto magnate Henry Ford paid $100,000 for the radio broadcast rights to the Series, which opened October 2 at Detroit's Navin Field (later renamed Tiger Stadium). To say they felt confident entering the affair was an understatement.

In addition to the momentum that came with just having completed the second-longest winning streak in major league history, Grimm's boys were sharp in every facet of the game. They played terrific defense. Their .288 club batting average—led by NL MVP Gabby Hartnett's .344 mark—paced the National League and was second only to Detroit's .290 in the majors. And their 3.26 team ERA was far and away tops in baseball, thanks to a fearsome starting rotation led by 20-game winners Warneke and Bill Lee. The Tigers, meanwhile, had never won a World Series championship.

Warneke got the Cubs started in dominant fashion, shutting out Detroit 3–0 in the opening game. The right-hander from Arkansas yielded only four hits and had all the run support he needed after his teammates plated two in the first inning. It looked as though Chicago's proven arms might be able to contain Detroit's potent bats.

However, as was the case many times throughout the Cubs' memorable season, things took a sudden turn. Game 2 starter Charlie Root, so impressive in a 15-win regular-season campaign, lasted just four batters during an 8–3 Detroit romp. The Tigers lost star slugger Hank

BILLY HERMAN (1931–1941)

When they named him WILLIAM JENNINGS BRYAN HERMAN in 1909, Billy Herman's parents may have had politics on their mind. But as it turned out, they had a different reason to be proud of their son. After 14 years as a celebrated second baseman, he won an election—to the National Baseball Hall of Fame in 1975.

Herman's baseball career began straight out of high school, with the Louisville Colonels in 1928. By the end of 1931, after a season marked by 59 RBIs and a .359 batting average, he was picked up by the Chicago Cubs for $50,000. He affirmed their faith in him by becoming an NL All-Star in 1934 and leading the league in both hits (227) and doubles (57) in 1935.

His decade-long career with the Cubs was stellar. The 5'11" right-hander was equally good as a hitter and a fielder. In fact, he set records at both. Herman was known for his skill with the "hit and run" play and holds the record for the most put-outs by a National League second baseman.

He batted higher than .300 in eight seasons (with a high of .341 in 1935) and was a National League All-Star 10 times. A down season offensively in 1940, however, resulted in a trade to the Dodgers.

Herman took a break from baseball in 1944 and 1945, serving in the navy during World War II. He played for another couple of years after his return before turning to coaching.

Billy Herman, on February 27, 1932.

Back in 1935, $6.60 would buy box seats at the World Series.

Greenberg to a fractured wrist during a home-plate collision in that victory, but it did not prevent them from seizing control in the Series' next two games.

Back at Wrigley, a pair of one-run thrillers gave Detroit a 3–1 Series lead. First, after the Cubs rallied for two runs in the bottom of the ninth to force extra innings in Game 3, the Tigers scored an unearned run in the 11th off left-hander Larry French to pull out a 6–5 nail-biter. Grimm and two of his players were ejected from that game for arguing calls made by umpire Larry Moriarty. Then, in Game 4, two Chicago errors in the sixth inning allowed Detroit to score the winning run in a 2–1 triumph over Tex Carleton. The Cubs found themselves in a deep hole.

Game 5 featured the return of Warneke to the mound for the Cubs, and it came not a moment too soon. Facing elimination in front of the home faithful, the Game 1 winner was every bit as untouchable as he had been in Detroit. He blanked the Tigers through six innings before leaving with shoulder pain. Lee mopped up to complete a 3–1 victory, the Cubs' first home World Series game win since 1918.

The loss failed to discourage the Detroiters. On the contrary, they were poised to celebrate their first world title knowing that the final two games—if it took that long—were back at their home park. They would only need one.

Game 6 was a classic. The Cubs' Billy Herman went 3-for-4 with a home run and drove in all three Chicago runs. The Tigers took leads of 1–0 and 2–1, but the Cubs produced two runs in the fifth for a 3–2 edge. Detroit came back with one in the sixth to tie the score in a game that featured 24 hits—a dozen for each side—despite the pitching arms of Detroit's Tommy Bridges and Chicago's French.

It came down to the ninth. Stan Hack led off the top of the inning with a triple, but the Cubs stranded him at third base thanks to some crafty pitching by Bridges. Then, in the bottom of the frame, Goose Goslin sent Detroit into a tizzy and gave the Tigers their first championship when he poked a two-out single to right field, scoring catcher/manager Mickey Cochrane to clinch it.

"This is the happiest day in my life," Cochrane said in the moments after the game. "It was the most sensational series I have ever played in. My greatest thrill was scoring that winning run."

Washington Redskins quarterback Sammy Baugh (No. 33) is brought down on the frozen Wrigley Field ground after a short gain against the Chicago Bears during the NFL Championship Game on December 12, 1937.

1937: SAMMY SLINGS REDSKINS TO NFL CROWN

"SLINGIN'" SAMMY BAUGH was no ordinary rookie in 1937. The Texas Christian All-American entered an NFL known for a conservative, pound-the-ball style and turned the league upside-down with his accurate arm. Baugh set an NFL record by completing 81 passes in his first season—the Redskins' first in Washington after moving from Boston.

By the end of the 1937 NFL Championship Game against George Halas' Bears on a frigid 15-degree day in Chicago, Baugh could barely walk. He was not the only one. Of the Wrigley Field conditions, Baugh said years later, "Every time you hit the frozen ground, you landed on little pebbles…you'd get scraped, and you'd be bleeding. It was a terrible day to play."

Still, Baugh and his teammates were not about to let a treacherous surface or a raucous Bears home crowd slow their high-flying attack. After Chicago took a 14–7 halftime lead on Jack Manders' second touchdown of the day, the Redskins came out firing in the second half.

Baugh threw touchdown passes covering 55, 78, and 35 yards to rally Washington to a 28–21 triumph. The first two went to the sensational Wayne

In the days before the Super Bowl, this 1937 poster touted the grandest football game of all, the "National Championship."

Millner, while Ed Justice hauled in the game winner in the fourth quarter. The Bears tried everything—sending more pressure up front and using an extra defensive back at various times—but nothing they tried could stop Baugh. After leading the NFL with slightly more than 100 passing yards per game during the regular season, Baugh threw for a remarkable 352 yards in the title game.

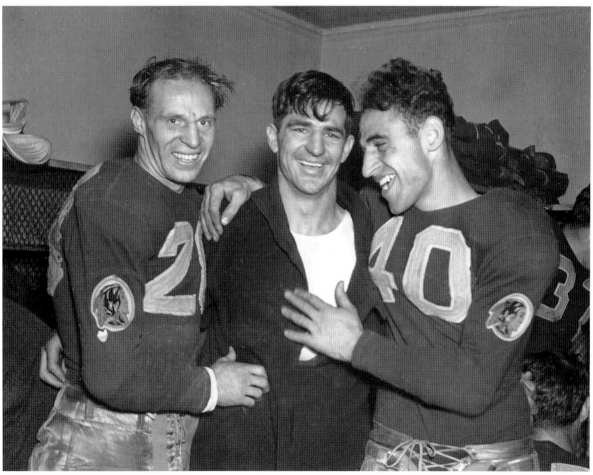

Quarterback Sammy Baugh, center, celebrates with teammates Cliff Battles, left, and Wayne Millner in the locker room after defeating the Chicago Bears at Wrigley Field in the NFL Championship Game on December 12, 1937.

THE CHICAGO CUBS
~1938~

LOGAN, HACK, BRYANT, EPPERLY, GALAN, MARTY, CARLETON, MATTICK
RUSSELL, JURGES, REYNOLDS, GARBARK, KIMBALL, LOTSHAW, DEAN, COLLINS, TRIPLETT, O'DEA, ASBELL
DEMAREE, LEE, FRENCH, LAZZERI, CORRIDEN, GRIMM, JOHNSON, HARTNETT, CAVARRETTA, HERMAN, ROOT
LAPORTA

The entire 1938 Cubs roster strikes a pose.

1938 WORLD SERIES: ROAMIN' IN THE GLOAMIN' ONE FOR THE AGES

*W*HEN THE MONTH of September began, few would have predicted that the game played on this Wednesday afternoon would provide perhaps the most memorable moment in Cubs history.

Many Cubs fans had given up on their team much earlier than September. On July 20, with the Cubs in fourth place, five and a half games behind league-leading Pittsburgh, owner P.K. Wrigley

fired manager Charlie Grimm and replaced him with catcher Gabby Hartnett. The change didn't help immediately: in the first 45 games with Hartnett as field boss, the Cubs went 23–22, the last two defeats coming in a September 3 doubleheader at Cincinnati. But then came a run reminiscent of 1935.

Charlie Root beat the Reds 2–1 in 11 innings on Sunday, September 4. And then, before 42,545 at Forbes Field, the Cubs swept a pair from the first-place Pirates. Bill Lee scattered 10 hits—three of them by future White Sox pitching coach Ray Berres—and won 3–0 in the opener. Later, Clay Bryant won his 15th game in Game 2 as the Cubs rallied for a 4–3 triumph. Even then, the Cubs were in third, five games back of the Bucs.

Next the North Siders swept three at St. Louis and went 4–3 against the Reds, Braves, Giants, and Dodgers before taking four straight at Philadelphia. The Cubs returned to Wrigley Field for a three-game series with St. Louis and swept it. They had won 17 of 20 and had moved into second place with a week to go, having closed to within 1 1/2 games of the Pirates, who had arrived in town for a three-game series that would determine the race's outcome.

To pitch the Tuesday opener, Hartnett selected Dizzy Dean, the sore-armed former St. Louis 30-game winner

Down one game to the Yankees, the Cubs called on the $185,000 arm of Dizzy Dean to stop the New York club in the second game of the World Series in Chicago on October 6, 1938. Diz (left) and manager Gabby Hartnett talk things over before the game.

Ann Hartnett, Gabby Hartnett's mom, was on hand for the first game of the World Series in Chicago against the Yankees on October 5, 1938, and she indicated what team she wanted to win when she gave Gabby this great big kiss.

who hadn't pitched in nine days and hadn't started since August 13. Lacking any semblance of a fastball but brimming with guts and guile, Dean, with last-out relief support from Lee, beat the Pirates 2–1 before 42,238, making the deficit a half-game.

The next afternoon, a partly cloudy one, it was Bryant, on two days' rest, against 30-year-old rookie right-hander Bob Klinger (12–5, 2.99 ERA in 1938), with 34,465 people in the stands. The Pirates scored three times in the sixth to take a 3–1 lead before the Cubs rallied to tie in their half, due in no small part to misplays in the outfield by Lloyd and Paul Waner. In the eighth, the Bucs went up 5–3 on RBI singles by Heinie Manush and Lee Handley, but again the Cubs came back to tie when pinch hitter Tony Lazzeri, the former Yankee, doubled in a run and Billy Herman singled home another. The bases soon were loaded with one out, but relief ace Mace Brown entered and got Frank Demaree to bounce into a double play.

Before the ninth inning began, the umpires, noting the growing darkness, met with the managers and told them that this would be the last inning, no matter what. If there was a tie, there would be a double-header instead of a single game the next day. Charlie Root, the sixth Cubs pitcher of the day, allowed a one-out single by Paul Waner, got Johnny Rizzo to pop out, and then received help from Hartnett, whose fine throw cut down Waner trying to steal second.

Then it was really getting dark. Phil Cavarretta began the Cubs' ninth and somehow saw enough of Brown's pitch to hit a fly ball to right for the first out. Carl Reynolds, whose 1938 numbers of three homers and a .302 batting average were a far cry from his 22 and .359 with the White Sox in 1930, was next and popped out. Then it was Hartnett, who took one curveball for a strike and swung at another and missed for strike two.

Then came another curveball. This time Hartnett didn't miss it.

"Hartnett didn't look good on either of the first two," Brown told sports columnist Dave Anderson years later. "I had a good curveball. I thought, *I'm going to strike him out with another curveball.* I wanted to throw it in the dirt, and he probably would've chased it. But I threw it high. If I had thrown him a fastball, he'd have taken it. But as soon as he hit it, I knew it was gone."

Gabby Hartnett knew it too. "I swung with everything I had," he told Anderson, "and then I got that kind of feeling you get when the blood rushes out of your head and you get dizzy."

The ball came down in the bleachers in left-center, touching off a home-plate celebration that included players, hundreds of fans, and dozens of ushers—who were supposed to keep the fans off the field but had failed.

Out in right field, Paul Waner watched in disbelief. "I just stood out there and watched Hartnett circle the bases and take the lousy pennant with him. That home run took all the fight out of us."

It also gave the Cubs a 6–5 victory and a half-game lead, which became $1^1/_2$ games when they routed the Bucs 10–1 on Thursday. Two days later, the Cubs clinched the pennant in St. Louis, and two days after that, an estimated 300,000 turned out for a parade through downtown Chicago to cheer the pennant winners—especially Gabby Hartnett.

ROGERS HORNSBY (1929–1931)

Awe-inspiring and jaw-dropping, ROGERS HORNSBY was as well known for his disagreeable temperament as for his accomplishments on the field. But when he was good, he was very, very good, and in Chicago he'll always be remembered for helping the Cubs win their first NL pennant after a decade-long drought.

Born in 1896, Hornsby loved baseball above all else. In a now-famous quote, the right-handed infielder was asked what he did all winter when there was no baseball. He replied that he spent it staring out the window—waiting for spring.

The Rajah of Swat—or simply Rajah— began his major league career with the Cardinals when he was just 19. He spent his first 12 years with the Cards, racking up accolades. By the time the Cubs acquired the right-handed phenom, he was a baseball legend. And he knew it. The Cubs coughed up five players and $200,000 cash to add him to their 1929 roster.

It was worth it—that year. A batting average of .380 combined with 149 RBIs, 156 runs scored, 39 home runs, and an MVP award made the man invaluable. The next year he broke his leg and was never the same.

The Cubs named Hornsby manager in 1930, and everything fell apart. He banned almost everything, making him the most hated man around. But he did enjoy gambling—and was in debt $11,000 to his own players. He was fired in 1931.

Hornsby earned seven batting titles and set an NL record with a .359 career batting average. He was inducted into the National Baseball Hall of Fame in 1942.

New Cubs manager Rogers "Rajah" Hornsby shakes hands with William Wrigley Jr., left, owner of the Chicago club, on September 25, 1930.

1941: WITH NATIONAL EYES ELSEWHERE, BEARS DEFEND TITLE

FOOTBALL WAS NOT foremost on the minds of Americans in December 1941. Two weeks after the Japanese attacked Pearl Harbor, Bears and Giants players put on their pads and readied for a game that would decide the NFL crown. They did so knowing that after the postgame handshakes, many of them would become teammates on a much more important field of battle.

The 1941 season was the first that featured a playoff game prior to the championship. That's because the Bears and Packers finished tied for first place in the Western Division. One week before the title match and one week after the attack that sent the United States headlong into World War II, Chicago turned back Green Bay 33–14 to earn a chance to defend its crown.

A mere 13,341 patrons—the smallest crowd in NFL Championship Game history—turned out at Wrigley Field for the December 21 title clash. What they witnessed was a one-sided contest in which their Bears more than doubled the Giants in yardage gained and took advantage of five turnovers in a 37–9 rout.

Bears quarterback Sid Luckman graces the cover of the official program of the 1941 "World's Championship" at Wrigley Field.

New York grabbed an early 6–3 edge on a Tuffy Leemans–to–George Franck touchdown pass and forged a 9–9 tie early in the third quarter. Chicago, though, pulled away with four unanswered touchdowns, owning the second half. Norm Standlee ran for two scores, Bob Snyder booted three first-half field goals, and Ken Kavanaugh closed the scoring on a 42-yard return of a Giants fumble.

The championship jewelry!

1943: A HEAPING DOSE OF BAD "LUCK" FOR REDSKINS

*J*UST ONE MONTH before the 1943 NFL Championship Game, Washington handed the Chicago Bears their only loss of the season. The Redskins trampled the Monsters of the Midway, rushing for 213 yards and forcing six turnovers in a 21–7 thumping in Washington, D.C. That was the first meeting between these fierce rivals since the Redskins had beaten the Bears for the 1942 NFL title.

The day after Christmas at Wrigley Field, however, the boys from Washington ran into an unstoppable force named Sid Luckman. Thus, there would be no third consecutive win over the Bears. The Chicago quarterback, coming off perhaps the best regular season in NFL history, turned in an unforgettable—and in many ways unparalleled—performance that drove the Bears to a 41–21 romp and their third NFL crown in four years.

Luckman, who averaged 220 passing yards and nearly three touchdown passes per game that year, hit 15-of-26 tosses for 276 yards and five TDs against Washington. He was the game's top rusher, rambling 64 yards—more than the Redskins mustered as a team—on just eight carries. He punted, returned punts, and twice intercepted Washington QB Sammy Baugh, returning those picks 33 yards. And after Washington took an early 7–0 edge, the Columbia University product steered his team to six of the game's next seven touchdowns. It's a wonder he didn't sing the national anthem and operate the scoreboard.

Right after the game, Luckman enlisted with the U.S. Merchant Marines. If the 1943 NFL Championship Game proved anything, it's that there was nothing this man could not do.

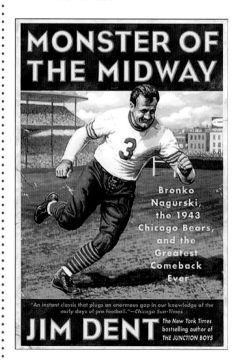

Bear Bronko Nagurski and the comeback in '43 were immortalized in this Jim Dent book.

Bears quarterback Sid Luckman warms up before a game against the Redskins on November 20, 1943.

With the championship being at the height of World War II, there is a plea to patriots at the bottom of the above program: "After reading this program…mail it to a man in service."

1945: BACK IN THE DRIVER'S SEAT

*W*HEN THE 1945 World Series matchup between the Chicago Cubs and the Detroit Tigers was set, Chicago sportswriter Warren Brown was asked for his prediction about the Series' outcome.

"I don't think either of them can win," Brown quipped.

The talent in the major leagues had been severely diluted because of World War II, and even though the war was over, many players still were completing their military service. Stan Musial of the Cardinals missed all of the 1945 season, one of the biggest reasons the Cubs were able to overtake St. Louis and win the NL pennant.

The Tigers players were on average older than many other teams and included slugging first baseman Hank Greenberg, who had rejoined the team after four years in the army when the war in Europe ended in May, and pitcher Virgil Trucks, who was discharged from the navy after the Japanese surrendered in August. Trucks returned in time to pitch the final game of the season, clinching the pennant.

Because of travel restrictions established during the war, the same restrictions that led to the cancellation of the 1945 All-Star Game, the first three

World War II had ended just a month before the '45 Series, but most of America's young men were not yet discharged from the army. It's no surprise that the bleachers were packed with men in uniform.

games of the Series were scheduled to be played in Detroit. Whatever remaining games were necessary would be played at Chicago's Wrigley Field.

That arrangement seemed to favor the Tigers, but those thoughts quickly disappeared when the Cubs roughed up ace Hal Newhouser in Game 1, rolling to a 9–0 victory.

A three-run homer by Greenberg carried the Tigers to a 4–1 victory in the second game, but Chicago regained the edge the next day when pitcher Claude Passeau threw a one-hitter in a 3–0 Cubs triumph. Only two Detroit batters reached base, Rudy York on a second-inning single and Bob Swift on a sixth-inning walk.

As the Series shifted to Chicago, the Cubs were only two victories away

The entire 1945 Cubs roster poses for this team photo.

The World Series pin bears the moniker "Victory World Series," though it had nothing to do with who won the ballgames. "Victory" is a reference to the allies winning the war over the Germans and Japanese.

from winning the World Series for the first time since 1908. Those two wins, however, proved elusive.

Before the fourth game, starlet June Haver visited both benches and planted a kiss on Cubs manager Charlie Grimm's cheek. Scalpers were getting as much as $200 for box seats, and grandstand seats were going for $75 a pair. Four men were even arrested before Game 5 trying to sell bleacher tickets for $5 and $6 each.

Unfortunately the Cubs did not give their fans much to cheer about in losing both Game 4 and Game 5. Detroit rode the pitching of Dizzy Trout to a 4–1 win in Game 4, and Newhouser bounced back with an 8–4 win in Game 5.

Needing a win in Game 6 to stay alive in the Series, the Cubs built a 7–3 lead in the eighth. Passeau was throwing another gem but had to come out of the game when he injured a finger trying to knock down a line drive in the seventh.

Relievers Hank Wyse and Ray Prim couldn't hold the lead, and the Tigers rallied for four runs in the eighth, capped by Greenberg's homer. The game went into extra innings. Hank Borowy, who had started and pitched five innings for the Cubs the day before, came out of the bullpen to throw four shutout innings as the teams battled until the 12th. Stan Hack's RBI double finally gave the Cubs the win, forcing the deciding Game 7. It was the last Series Game 7 in the history of the Cubs franchise.

The excitement in Chicago was at a fever pitch. The more than 36,000 reserved seats sold out in three and a half hours, making it only the second pregame sellout of a Game 7 in history.

Excitement was not just limited to Chicago. The games were broadcast around the world by the Armed Forces Radio Network, and many soldiers reportedly rose at 3:00 AM in the Philippines to listen to the broadcasts. For the first time since 1941, players shared in the $100,000 fee paid by the Gillette Safety Razor Blade Co. to sponsor the radio broadcasts. For the previous three years, that money had been added to baseball's contribution to the war charities and funds.

The familiar marquee in front of Wrigley Field had an unfamiliar message—"National League Champions"—at least during the 1940s.

The win in Game 6 proved costly for the Cubs, however, as Borowy had been manager Charlie Grimm's expected starter in Game 7. The teams had a day of rest between Games 6 and 7, and Grimm decided to go with Borowy as his starter anyway.

It was immediately obvious that Borowy was out of gas, and after the first three Detroit batters all reached on singles, Grimm pulled Borowy and brought in Paul Derringer, but he proved to be almost as ineffective. The Tigers scored five runs in the first inning, deflating the crowd of 41,590 almost before they had a chance to get settled in their seats.

The final score was 9–3. Newhouser, pitching on two days' rest, scattered 10 hits in cruising to the victory and extending the Cubs' streak without a world championship for another year.

"We were beaten by a good club, but not a better club than I have," Grimm

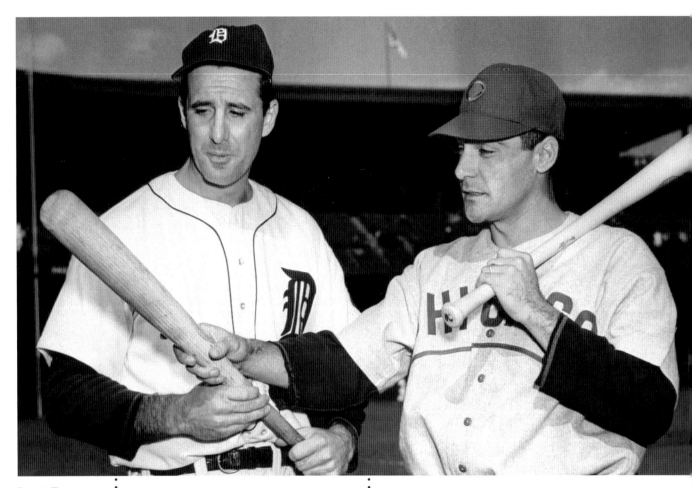

Detroit Tigers left fielder Hank Greenberg, left, and Chicago Cubs first baseman Phil Cavarretta, right, whose powerful bats were a deciding factor in the Cubs' victories in Games 1, 3, and 6.

said. "Just pitching beat us, but these guys are still champs in my book. They gave it everything they had.

"Borowy didn't have a lot when he warmed up and I knew it, but I wanted to give it a try. I thought maybe he'd get by until he warmed up to the job."

That didn't happen, however, and Cubs fans were forced to spend yet another winter lamenting how close they had come to victory. They didn't know their wait for a championship was really only just beginning.

1945: CURSE OF THE BILLY GOAT

DID THE CUBS lose the 1945 World Series because of a curse?

When the Series shifted to Chicago for Game 4, a man named William Sianis, who owned a popular tavern, had two box-seat tickets for the game and brought his pet goat with him as his guest. The ushers tried to keep Sianis and the goat out of the ballpark, but he made it inside and actually paraded the goat around on the field. Sianis pinned a note on the goat that said "We've Got Detroit's Goat."

During the game, Cubs owner Phil Wrigley found out what was going on, apparently when the smell from the goat made it up to the owner's box, and had Sianis and the goat ejected from the stadium. Before he left the stadium, Sianis reportedly put a curse on the Cubs that said the team would never win another pennant or play in another World Series.

After the Tigers won the deciding Game 7 of the Series, Sianis reportedly sent a telegram to Wrigley that read, Who SMELLS NOW?

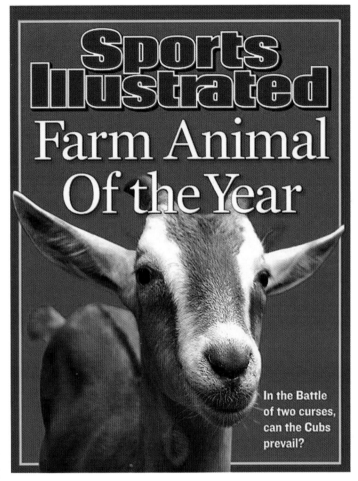

This magazine cover that was published decades after the 1945 "curse" is a testament to the endurance of the legend of the goat.

William "Billy Goat" Sianis, tavern proprietor, watches his four-legged pet duck, Victory, gulp a billful of beer in Chicago on November 12, 1945. The duck has two normal legs and two short legs behind them that are used for scratching purposes.

The 1947 All-Star Game media badge issued by Wrigley Field and provided to all the reporters and newspaper writers who would be covering the game.

The Postwar Years Through the 1970s

Many amazing things continued to happen at Wrigley from the end of the Depression through the 1970s, including Stan Musial's 3,000th hit, several no-hitters by Cubs pitchers, and lots of Chicago Bears action!

1947: AL PREVAILS IN ALL-STAR NAIL-BITER

IT WAS A Chicagoan responsible for the existence of the Major League Baseball All-Star Game. Arch Ward, longtime sports editor of the *Chicago Tribune*, lobbied during the Great Depression for a game pitting the best players from each league against each other. "Baseball needs to show that it is not in a state of decadence," Ward argued. The result, in 1933, was the very first MLB All-Star Game and the beginning of a tradition that carries on to this day.

Fourteen years after Comiskey Park hosted that inaugural Midsummer Classic on the South Side, the event returned to Chicago on July 8, 1947. More than 41,000 fans jammed the North Side's Wrigley Field to watch the best players in the game show off their skills, but folks from all over America had already put their stamp on the proceedings. That's because 1947 was the first year in which the American and National League's starting lineups—except pitchers—were determined by a nationwide fan vote.

Known throughout the years as a "hitter's park," Wrigley was nothing of the sort on this summer day. Pitchers dominated this game. Starting hurlers Hal Newhouser of the AL and Ewell Blackwell of the NL both threw one-hit shutout ball over their three-inning stints. It wasn't until the fourth inning that Giants star Johnny

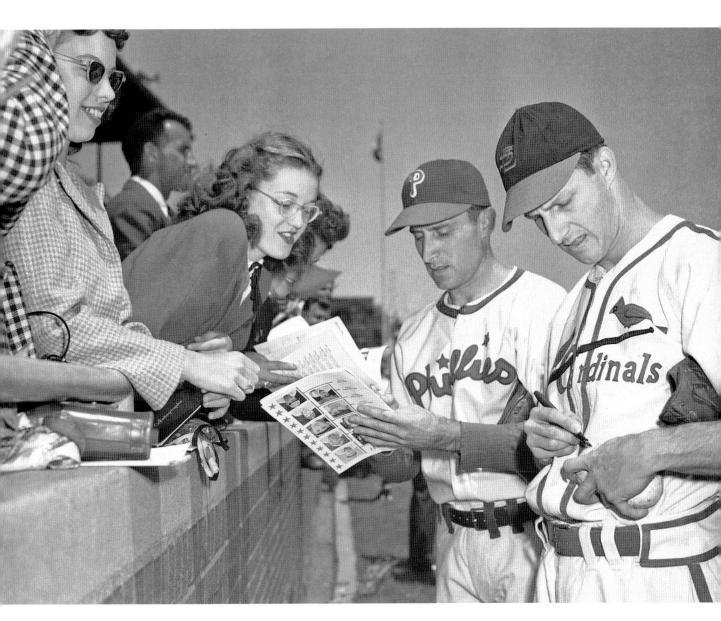

Stan Musial, right, and Emil Verban of the National League All-Star team oblige fans at Wrigley Field on July 8, 1947, by autographing baseballs and programs before the start of the game against the American League All-Stars.

ALL STAR SOUVENIR PROGRAM 25¢

WRIGLEY FIELD · CHICAGO 1947

Though World War II had ended two years before the '47 All-Star Game, the program still had patriotic references.

runs in the later innings. Luke Appling trotted home from third base with the tying run in the sixth when Yankees great Joe DiMaggio grounded into a double play. Then, in the seventh, Bobby Doerr singled, stole second base, took third on an errant pickoff attempt, and scored what turned out to be the winning run in a 2–1 AL victory on Stan Spence's single. It made Shea the first rookie pitcher to capture an All-Star Game victory.

Despite the loss by the NL, Chicago fans got to cheer on a couple of their local heroes during Wrigley Field's All-Star Game debut. Cubs center fielder Andy Pafko, a reserve, provided one of just five National League hits off four different AL pitchers when he singled to center in the fifth inning. And Phil Cavarretta, the other North Sider on the NL roster, entered the game as a pinch hitter in the eighth inning but struck out against Walt Masterson.

Masterson gave way to Joe Page in the ninth inning, and the NL put the potential tying run on base when Pee Wee Reese drew a one-out walk. Any drama ended there, however, as a routine grounder and a fly ball by the next two hitters put a bow on the AL's second consecutive All-Star Game victory. Up in the press box, Chicago's favorite sports editor was surely smiling.

Mize belted a home run over the ivy-covered right-field wall off rookie reliever Frank "Spec" Shea to give the NL a 1–0 lead.

Shea was unblemished over the remainder of his three-inning stint, however, and wound up earning the victory when his AL teammates scratched out two

1950: FROM "OH NO" TO "NO-NO," JONES TOSSES GEM

S AM JONES HAD two nicknames. Most called him "Toothpick," a reference to the fact that he rolled a toothpick between his teeth when he pitched. Some were also fond of calling the Cubs starter "Sad Sam," a nod to the fact that he seemed to wear a perennial pout on his face.

Hank Aaron, who retired as the most prolific home-run hitter in major league history, had a vastly different recollection of Jones. Hammerin' Hank recalled him as the hurler who made him look foolish at the plate during a game at Wrigley Field. "I remember my third year, I faced Sam Jones and he struck me out three times in Chicago," Aaron told talk-show host David Letterman. "That was the most embarrassing feeling in the world."

If Jones could rack up strikeouts, he could also pile up walks—much to the chagrin of his managers. From 1955 to 1959, the towering right-hander from Ohio led the National League four times in walks allowed. His penchant for wildness was never on better display than during his greatest day on the mound.

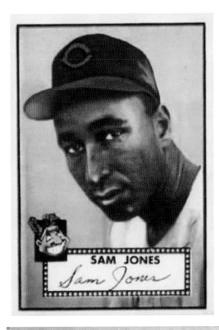

Back in the early 1950s, no respectable baseball card collection would be without this one!

SAM JONES

Cub Negro Strikes Out Side in 9th

3 Bucs Stranded As Game Ends, 4-0

1950 was long before headline writers were "politically correct."

Sam Jones in March 1956.

The date was May 12, 1955, an early season game during the first year he led the NL in free passes. Pittsburgh was visiting Wrigley Field on a cold Thursday afternoon, and a mere 2,918 fans turned out to watch. Jones was his usual self in many ways, firing live heaters and dastardly curveballs all over the place. "If you were a right-handed hitter, that ball was a good four feet behind you," Hoby Landrith once said of Jones' curve. "It took a little courage to stay in there, because he was wild."

But Jones was something else on that day. At least to the Pirates, he was flat-out unhittable. Through eight innings, he walked four batters and struck out three while not allowing a base hit. Jones took a 4–0 lead into the top of the ninth inning, and what fans remained in the house were on their feet, ready to celebrate a no-hitter.

It would not come easily, and Jones had no one to blame but himself. He opened the inning by walking Gene Freese, Preston Ward, and Tom Saffell, with a wild pitch mixed in for good measure. At that point, with the bases loaded and the heart of the Pirates order due up, Cubs skipper Stan Hack was not thinking about preserving a no-hitter, but about trying to hang on to a victory as he strolled to the mound for a visit.

Hack asked Jones if he was tired. When the answer was no, Hack said, "Well, then, Sam, how about getting some of those pitches over the plate?" Jones then did precisely that. He was as dominant pitching to the last three batters of the inning as he was wild against the first three. He struck out Dick Groat looking, Roberto Clemente swinging, and Frank Thomas, looking to complete the first no-hitter at Wrigley field since 1917 and the first in major league history by an African American pitcher.

ERNIE BANKS' teams had a losing record in 13 of his first 14 seasons, and he never played in the postseason. Yet through it all, "Mr. Cub," as he came to be known, embodied the unbreakable spirit of the Cubs fans as its greatest player in franchise history.

The Dallas native got his professional start with the Kansas City Monarchs in the Negro Leagues. The legendary Buck O'Neil signed him for the Cubs, and in 1953, Banks broke the color line with the team along with Gene Baker, who had been signed from the Monarchs a few years earlier and was in the Cubs' minor league system. Banks wore No. 14, played shortstop, and quickly wowed both teammates and fans with his powerful swing.

In his second full season in 1955, Banks pounded 44 home runs, five of which were grand slams. After hitting "only" 28 in 1956, Banks went on a tear, hitting 43, 47, 45, and 41 round-trippers the next four seasons. His 1958 campaign was one to behold—47 homers and 129 RBIs en route to the MVP, followed by 45 homers and 143 RBIs in 1959 as he became the first player to repeat as the National League's Most Valuable Player.

In 1962 Banks made the move to first base but continued his steady presence in the middle of the Cubs' batting order, averaging 25 homers each year for the rest of the decade. His last big year was in 1969, with 23 homers and 106 runs batted in. In 1970 he became the first Cub and only the ninth player at the time to reach the 500-home-run plateau. He retired in 1971 after 14 All-Star appearances, the most of any Cubs player.

Banks was a first-ballot Hall of Famer in 1977. In 1982 Banks' No. 14 was the first Cubs jersey to be retired. He was named to Major League Baseball's All-Century Team in 1999. In 2008 the Cubs unveiled a statue of Banks outside Wrigley Field.

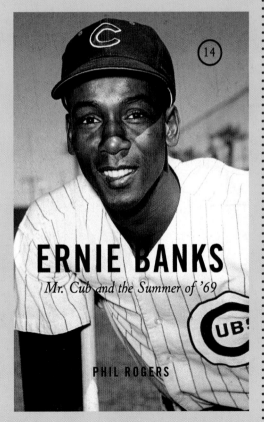

ERNIE BANKS
Mr. Cub and the Summer of '69

PHIL ROGERS

ERNIE BANKS
(1953–1971)

THE NO. 1 ST. LOUIS WEBSITE AND NEWSPAPER

FINAL EDITION • SUNDAY • 1.20.2013 • $2.50

SUNDAY POST-DISPATCH

1920 § 2013

Stan Musial

The greatest Cardinal ushered in an era of sustained success. But it was his kindness and approachability that made him an enduring civic treasure.

IN THIS PAPER • 14-PAGE SPECIAL SECTION LOOKS AT HIS LIFE AND CAREER • SECTION S

The "weight" of this headline and the giant photo emblazoned across the front page of the *St. Louis Post-Dispatch* speaks volumes about the importance of Stan the Man in his hometown, though his 3,000th hit was achieved 300 miles away in Chicago, at Wrigley Field!

1958: STAN THE MAN JOINS 3,000-HIT CLUB

RARE IS THE day Chicago Cubs fans get off their seats to cheer for a Cardinal at Wrigley Field. Rare was the day Cardinals slugger Stan "the Man" Musial was not penciled in to the starting lineup. May 13, 1958, just happened to be such a day—on both counts—as Musial recorded his 3,000th hit in dramatic fashion.

St. Louis manager Fred Hutchinson had not intended to play Musial in a series finale in Chicago, hoping that Musial could reach the milestone once the team returned home. However, with the Cardinals trailing 3–1 in the sixth inning and their five-game winning streak in jeopardy, Musial came striding in from the Cardinals bullpen, where he had been enjoying the afternoon sun on a green folding chair.

His entrance earned a polite cheer from the small crowd of Cubs fans—slightly more than 5,000 in number—but what happened next drew a roar. Pinch-hitting against Moe Drabowsky, some 15 years his junior, Musial crushed a double into the left-field corner. It scored Gene Green with the Cardinals' second run of the game, sparked a four-run rally that

The Sporting News, though nationally circulated, is edited and published in St. Louis. It's no surprise they touted Musial's achievement on the front page!

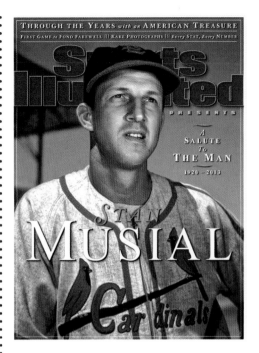

Though absent from baseball for many decades now, the legacy of Stan the Man continues to this day.

led St. Louis to victory, and caused minor mayhem at the Friendly Confines.

Fans screamed and shouted. Photographers jumped out of their designated areas and spilled onto the field, capturing the moment from every angle. Umpire Frank Dascoli retrieved the baseball and jogged it over to Musial, shaking his hand. Hutchinson posed at second base with his star hitting machine, who became just the eighth player in history to reach 3,000 hits.

"It isn't every day a man gets his 3,000th hit," said the Man, who accomplished the feat in less time than any of his seven predecessors, beating Ty Cobb by three months. "I'm glad it was a good, clean shot."

Hutchinson removed Musial for a pinch runner before play resumed, a move that could have come back to haunt the manager had the game required another key Cardinals hit in the later innings. As it happened, St. Louis tacked on three more runs for a 5–3 victory over their Chicago rivals,

Stan "the Man" Musial holds a silver bat as four of his guests hold up the number 3,000 at a party given in honor of Musial's imminent 3,000th hit. At the time of this photo he was at 2,998.

and the Cardinals' celebration continued on a raucous train ride back to St. Louis.

The Illinois Central Railroad provided a cake adorned with the number 3,000 in red frosting for the joyous ride home. Harry Caray, then the Cardinals' announcer—who would later call Wrigley Field his home field as legendary Cubs broadcaster—presented Stan a pair of diamond cufflinks commemorating the achievement. Musial stepped off the train at a quick stop in Springfield, Illinois, to sign autographs for fans there. And when his party on wheels finally pulled into Union Station in St. Louis, hundreds of Cardinals fans greeted their hero.

Offered Musial, "Ranking with such great hitters helps make this my greatest thrill, even more than my seven batting championships or [The Sporting News] Player of the Decade Award." Not a bad day for a guy who wasn't supposed to be in the lineup.

The late LOU BOUDREAU was the voice of the Chicago Cubs on WGN Radio and Television from 1958 until 1988, with a break from the broadcast booth during the 1960 season, when he managed the Cubbies. Among the best color commentators, Boudreau is a native of Harvey, Illinois, a suburb of the Windy City. His reputation as a "stat man" and fount of baseball knowledge was acclaimed.

Known as a strategic thinker, he was instrumental in moving Ron Santo from catcher to third base. Earlier, as the manager of the Cleveland Indians, he switched Hall of Famer Bob Lemon from the outfielder to the mound. He also created "the Boudreau Shift," used against famous pull-hitter Ted Williams of the Boston Red Sox. The "shift" strategy was to blanket the right side of the field to thwart left-handed batters. It was later copied by many other ballclubs and still is in use today.

His 15-year career on the diamond earned Boudreau induction into the National Baseball Hall of Fame in 1970. As a player and manager with the Cleveland Indians, he piloted the team to win the 1948 World Series as the youngest player-manager in baseball history. That same year, he was voted the American League Most Valuable Player and was an eight-time All-Star. He eventually managed the Boston Red Sox from 1952 to 1954 and the Kansas City Athletics from 1955 to 1957.

One of his most endearing qualities was his use of the term "good kid," which he frequently called fans. He felt these two simple words eliminated the uneasiness of not knowing the names of everyone he spoke with. Later, he even began to address his own children as "good kid," which was one of their fondest memories of their legendary father.

Baseball and heroics ran in the Boudreau family. His daughter Sharon married MVP and Cy Young Award–winning pitcher Denny McClain; youngest son Jim was a Triple-A pitcher for the Cubs organization; and oldest son Lou Jr. did play-by-play for the Memphis Blues, Triple A Affiliate of the Houston Astros. Lou Jr. is also an ex-marine who saw combat and was wounded in Vietnam.

LOU BOUDREAU—CUBS MANAGER, WGN BROADCASTER (1958–1988)

This Cardwell baseball card all of a sudden had new meaning—he was a no-hitter pitcher! And with so little good news to report about the Cubs, it's no wonder the newspaper at right made it a front-page story!

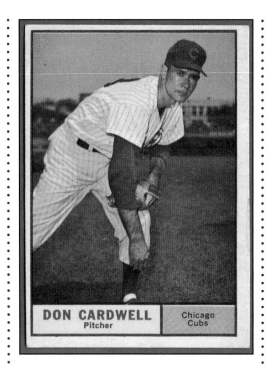

DON CARDWELL
Pitcher

Chicago Cubs

1960: THE NEW KID IN TOWN

IT DID NOT take newcomer Don Cardwell long to become popular among his Chicago Cubs teammates. Just two days after being acquired in a trade with the Phillies, the canon-armed 24-year-old was slated to start the second game of a May 15, 1960, double-header against the Cardinals at Wrigley Field. While some might have succumbed to the pressure of leading a new team against a vaunted rival, Cardwell took it in stride as he faced the Cardinals.

Carrying his Phillies gym bag to the park, Cardwell—needless to say—was still getting used to his surroundings. Before the game, he and catcher Del Rice agreed that they would not use Cardwell's slider, but would rather rely mainly on fastballs while getting to know each other. It turned out to be a brilliant strategy. Although Cardwell walked the second batter of the game, the right-hander quickly settled into a groove and began firing bullets that the St. Louis hitters struggled to handle.

Cardwell did not walk another man all day, while striking out seven. He entered the ninth inning with a 4–0 lead, having not allowed a hit—three batters away from baseball immortality. The 33,543 fans were on their feet as the Cardinals sent Carl Sawatski to the plate. With a 1–2 count, the pinch hitter fired a rocket out to right field. George Altman sprinted all the way to the warning track and made a leaping catch, the first of two fine defensive plays by the Cubs in the inning. Another pinch hitter, George Crowe, got ahead in the count but was fooled on a 2–0 pitch and sent a lazy fly to center. Two outs.

Joe Cunningham, the Cardinals leadoff man, stepped into the batter's box and worked for a favorable 3–1 count in his effort to extend the game and keep Cardwell from making history. Umpire Tony Venzon called the next pitch, a laser beam at Cunningham's knees, strike two and quickly caught an earful from the batter. "And here is Cunningham hollering his head off," shouted Cubs broadcaster Jack Brickhouse, relaying the suspense to his listeners. "Ball Three. Strike Two. Two outs. Ninth inning."

After picking up a handful of dirt and rubbing his hands together, Cunningham stepped in to face the full count. What unfolded next seemed nothing short of miraculous. Cunningham lined Cardwell's final fastball of the afternoon sharply to left field. That's where Walt "Moose" Moryn, a 6'2", 220-pound beast, came lumbering in to make a game-ending shoestring catch that would define his career.

All Cardwell could do was stand and watch. "He made me famous," the pitcher said of Moryn. "After I threw the pitch, I was leaning down with him and saying, 'C'mon, Moose, make the catch.'" While neither Cardwell nor the Cubs went on to enjoy a great season (the former went 8–14 during a 60–94 year for the Cubs), they provided a shining moment in Cubs and Wrigley Field history: the only no-hitter thrown by a pitcher in his first appearance after being traded.

The most striking thing today about this 50-year-old championship ticket stub is surely its price: $10.

This championship program makes reference to what Yogi Berra might call "déjà vu all over again," with the Bears and the Giants facing off again for the world title, exactly 50 years after they dueled for it in 1933.

1963: CHICAGO DEFENSE "BEARS" DOWN

NO STRANGER TO NFL Championship Game heroics, former Chicago quarterbacking great Sid Luckman—an assistant coach for the 1963 squad—predicted a classic between the Giants and Bears on December 29, 1963, at Wrigley Field. He said, "[It] figures to be one of the best in history… because you've got the Bears' great defense against the Giants' great offense."

It had been 17 years since Chicago had last won the crown, and the Windy City faithful were ready to celebrate. More than 45,000 turned out to watch their Western Conference champs tangle with a Giants juggernaut that had averaged 32 points per game behind the arm of Y.A. Tittle.

Chicago boss George Halas and defensive coordinator George Allen favored a smashmouth approach, and their Bears succeeded in coaxing a defensive clash. Single-digit temperatures with a sub-zero wind chill helped, causing every hit to hurt a little more and adding difficulty to the Giants' passing game.

Tittle hit Frank Gifford with a 14-yard pass to open the scoring but was hit in the knee by linebacker Larry Morris on the play. It was only the beginning of a painful day for Tittle, who threw an uncharacteristic five interceptions.

Chicago's Billy Wade scored on a QB sneak for a 7–7 tie in the final seconds of the opening quarter, but the Giants reclaimed the lead, 10–7, before halftime. Tittle, however, was hurting. Another shot to the knee from Morris caused a *pop* late in the second quarter, and the star QB was not the same thereafter.

Wade bulled over the goal line again in the third quarter, and the Bears defense took it from there, shutting out the Giants in the second half for a 14–10 victory that brought the NFL title back to Chicago.

A view from high above Wrigley Field just before kickoff of the championship game between the Chicago Bears and the New York Giants on December 29, 1963.

1965: ROOKIE SAYERS CUTS THROUGH MUD FOR RECORD SIX TDS

A brightly colored banner for a banner year in the playing career of Bears great Gayle Sayers.

GIVE HIM A field to run on, and no one did it better than Gale "the Kansas Comet" Sayers. Though injuries limited his Hall of Fame career to seven seasons, he caused more headaches for defensive players than most running backs could dream of doing in a lifetime. "There was a magic about him that still sets him apart from the other great running backs," wrote the great Red Smith. "He wasn't a bruiser like Jimmy Brown, but he could slice through the middle like a warm knife through butter, and when he took a pitchout and peeled around the corner, he was the most exciting thing in pro football."

During his 1965 rookie campaign, Sayers showed that—actually—a field wasn't necessarily a prerequisite. Wrigley Field was a messy mud pit on December 12 when the San Francisco 49ers came to town. Players were slipping and sliding everywhere, with one exception: the Kansas Comet. Sayers squirmed through seemingly every hole and dodged every would-be tackler on his way to an NFL record–tying six touchdowns.

He caught a screen pass from Rudy Bukich in the opening quarter and raced 80 yards to the end zone for his first score. In the second quarter, Sayers got loose on scoring scampers covering 21 and seven yards to lift the Bears to a 27–13 halftime lead. He later remarked that he must have been the only man on the field that afternoon who managed to find his footing in the slop.

The 49ers had routed the Bears 54–24 earlier that season, holding Sayers to just 44 yards on 12 carries in his NFL debut.

The AP named Bears rookie Gale Sayers Offensive Player of the Week on October 19, 1965, for his performance (four touchdowns!) in the Bears' October 17, 1965, victory over the Minnesota Vikings.

On this day, though, they had no answer for the former Kansas All-American.

Sayers broke through the line and dashed 50 yards to open the second-half scoring, and plunged in from the 1 for his fifth touchdown later in the quarter as the Bears pulled away for a 40–13 lead. The comfortable gap resulted in Bears coach George Halas putting Sayers and several other starters on the bench.

However, Sayers lobbied to get back in the game, and eventually Halas obliged. Papa Bear put his rookie phenom back in to field a fourth-quarter punt, and Sayers returned it 85 yards on a dazzling play for his NFL record–tying sixth touchdown of the game. It matched a feat first accomplished by Ernie Nevers in 1929 and equaled by Dub Jones 22 years later. Realistically, Sayers could have crossed the goal line at least another time or two, but the 61–20 final margin limited his second-half contributions.

In all, Sayers carried the ball just nine times for 113 yards and four TDs. He caught two passes for 89 yards and a score. Throw in his five punt returns, and he touched the ball only 16 times in the game while covering 336 yards—21 yards a touch. The six touchdowns brought his season total to 21, another NFL record. Sayers added a 22nd in the season finale the next week, establishing an NFL record that stood for a decade.

APRIL 8, 1969: WILLIE SMITH'S OPENING DAY HEROICS

IT'S FITTING THAT one of the most memorable seasons in Cubs history would begin with one of the most memorable games.

The Willie Smith Game: it's the only description needed. And in Philadelphia it might be remembered as the Don Money Game if fate hadn't intervened in the person of Willie Smith, a cheerful, amiable pitcher-turned-outfielder who also sang professionally during a fairly obscure baseball career that featured one unforgettable moment.

The 1969 season was the Cubs' fourth under firebrand manager Leo Durocher. They had improved in each of the previous three campaigns after ruefully living up to Durocher's takeover pronouncement that "this is not an eighth-place team" by finishing 10th in 1966.

Even before it started, the 1969 season was historic. Expansion added two teams to each league—Montreal and San Diego in the National League, Kansas City and Seattle in the American—and four six-team divisions were created to facilitate scheduling and emphasize geographical rivalries. The schedule remained at 162 games, with the division champions then meeting in two best-of-five playoff series to determine each league's World Series representative.

The Cubs were assigned to the National League East, one of the toughest divisions, with the two-time pennant-winning Cardinals, the hard-hitting Pirates, and on-the-rise young clubs in the New York Mets and Philadelphia. But the Cubs were a confident team when they took the field for the April 8 season opener against the Phillies, and a standing-room crowd of 40,796 at Wrigley Field shared in that optimism.

Ernie Banks was still Mr. Cub, still a productive, dangerous hitter at 38. All-Stars Billy Williams, 30, and Ron Santo, 29, added more thunder to the middle of an imposing batting order. Young veterans Glenn Beckert and Don Kessinger joined Santo and Banks in the league's best infield. Randy Hundley was a rock behind the plate and deft handler of a pitching staff that featured Fergie Jenkins, Ken Holtzman, and Bill Hands in a strong rotation.

The bench, the bullpen, and rookie Don Young in center field were the team's only question marks, but nobody wanted to hear a discouraging word on Opening Day. The call to "Play ball!" produced spine-tingling anticipation.

A single, a sacrifice, his own error, and Deron Johnson's RBI single put Jenkins in a 1–0 hole in the first inning,

Willie Smith | OUTFIELD

On Opening Day in 1969, this Willie Smith baseball card was ho-hum; by the next day, it was a memento of the man who started the '69 drive to the pennant, though the Cubs never quite got there in the end.

but Banks got him out of it when he powered a three-run homer into the left-field bleachers off Chris Short in the bottom of the first.

It remained a 3–1 game when Banks faced Short with Williams on first and one out in the bottom of the third. Banks took the veteran lefty deep again for a 5–1 lead as Wrigley rocked.

Jenkins had a propensity for giving up solo homers throughout his career, so no one flinched when the rookie Don Money tagged him for one leading off the seventh inning, cutting the Cubs' lead to 5–2. Jenkins settled down and was three

By midseason 1969, this autographed picture of Willie Smith was a treasure and a keepsake. He was the man who kicked off the best Cubs season since World War II.

manager Bob Skinner demonstrated his faith in the rookie right-hander by letting him bat in the 11th, after an RBI double by Money had given the Phils a 6–5 lead. Money was 3-for-5 with 10 total bases and five RBIs for the day.

Lersch stayed in the game and got Banks on a fly to right, leading off the 11th, then gave up a single to Hundley. With Jim Hickman due up, Durocher played one of the hunches for which he was famous. Hickman was 0-for-4 with a strikeout, and Durocher didn't like his chances against the hard-throwing Lersch in the gathering dusk. So he went to his bench for the left-handed-hitting Smith, a former pitcher who'd been converted into an outfielder while playing for the Angels because of how well he swung the bat.

Smith, 30, had one thing in mind as he stepped to the plate with darkness falling. And when Lersch threw him a 1–1 fastball, he produced it, sending a high drive into the right-field bleachers. The game-winning two-run pinch-hit homer touched off pandemonium at Wrigley Field. Hundley fairly danced around the bases in front of Smith. Jack Brickhouse's call on television—"Willie Smith!!! Willie Smith!!!"—was simple but eloquent, one of the most memorable in Brickhouse's Hall of Fame career. Throughout Chicago there was a sense that this could be the start of something big.

outs away from a complete-game victory when Johnny Callison and Cookie Rojas opened the ninth inning with singles. That brought Money to the plate, and the 22-year-old shortstop was money once again, slamming a three-run homer off Jenkins that tied the game 5–5 and turned the raucous crowd deathly quiet.

Barry Lersch, in his major league debut, had shut down the Cubs on two hits over four innings in relief, and Phillies

The quiet Hall of Famer from Whistler, Alabama, is a six-time All-Star. From 1962 until 1971, BILLY WILLIAMS appeared in a National League–record 1,117 consecutive games. The 1961 NL Rookie of the Year also hit at least 20 homers 13 years in a row, ending his career with 426 home runs.

Williams had a monster season in 1970 with 205 hits, a .322 average, 42 homers, 129 RBIs, and 137 runs scored, but finished second to Johnny Bench in the MVP voting. Williams won the National League batting title in 1972 with a .333 average, added 37 homers and 122 RBIs, but lost the MVP vote to Bench again that year.

"Billy was one of the sweetest-swinging left-handed hitters I've ever seen," said Ron Santo, who played with him in the minors. "He had such quick hands, a lot like Ernie [Banks]. You know, Billy was quiet, but he spoke his mind. He was a leader. He wasn't a guy to just sit back."

In 1975 Williams was traded for Manny Trillo and spent his final two years in Oakland, then retired after the 1976 season. After being snubbed in five straight elections, the baseball writers finally saw the light and elected him to the Hall of Fame in 1987. His No. 26 was retired by the Cubs that same year and still flies atop the right-field foul pole. Williams has remained with the team as a special assistant and is always a popular presence in the dugout and around the batting cage before games.

BILLY WILLIAMS
(1959–1974)

The feeling lasted throughout the summer as the Cubs played championship-caliber baseball, drew record crowds to Wrigley Field, and turned their "Bleacher Bum" followers into cult figures. The end of their World Series drought—then a modest 24 years—seemed to be in sight.

But it was not to be. Their lack of depth exposed the Cubs as a tired team in the season's final six weeks. Meanwhile, the Mets caught fire behind a dominant young pitching staff. They not only overtook the Cubs to win the NL East, they swept the Atlanta Braves in the first National League Championship Series and stunned the heavily favored Baltimore Orioles in a five-game World Series, earning a place in baseball lore as the "Miracle Mets."

History is less kind to the Cubs. Their 92–70 record and second-place finish is viewed as an epic collapse, and there's no denying it was a dispiriting letdown, mostly because of the day-to-day thrills and high-wire excitement that preceded it. But no one who experienced that 1969 season will ever forget it, least of all Willie Smith.

He died of a heart attack in his hometown of Anniston, Alabama, in 2006. He was 66. He had modest numbers: a .248 career batting average, 46 home runs, 211 RBIs…and one moment that will live forever in Cubs history.

JUNE 29, 1969: BILLY WILLIAMS DAY

IT'S UNUSUAL FOR a team to salute a player with an official "day" unless that player is on a victory lap as he nears retirement or has already moved on.

Billy Williams was 31 when the Cubs honored him with Billy Williams Day between games of a Sunday doubleheader at Wrigley Field, and some of his best baseball years were still to come. But he was on the cusp of a significant milestone. In starting the first game, Williams tied Stan Musial's National League record for consecutive games played, with 896. He broke Stan the Man's record in the second game.

Before the largest Wrigley crowd of the season, 41,060, the Cubs celebrated by beating Musial's former team twice. The man of the hour rose to the occasion with two doubles, two triples, five hits, and three RBIs.

"It was easily my biggest day in all my years with the Cubs," Williams said.

On September 21, 1963, manager Bob Kennedy decided to sit Williams against the Milwaukee Braves' Warren Spahn, a tough left-hander. Billy Cowan was the Cubs' left fielder, with Nelson Mathews in center and Ellis Burton in right. Williams was back in the lineup the next day, and he didn't miss another game until September 3, 1970, when he told manager Leo Durocher it was time for a break.

Williams had perfect attendance for 1,117 games over seven years, along with Hall of Fame–caliber hitting and outfield play.

"Billy Williams, day in and day out, is the best hitter I've ever seen," teammate Don Kessinger said. "He didn't hit for one or two days, or one or two weeks. He hit all the time."

True, but sometimes it took a while when Bob Gibson was pitching. Williams was 0-for-3 against the Cardinals' hard-eyed ace when he came to bat in the eighth inning of the opener and whaled a double off the wall in left-center field. One out later, Ernie Banks stroked a single to center, scoring Williams with the first run of the game. When Willie Smith followed with a two-run bomb onto Sheffield Avenue, Fergie Jenkins had all the support he'd need to beat Gibson in one of their classic pitching duels, this one completed in a crisp two hours, six minutes.

The Cubs took all the suspense out of the second game with a four-run first inning. Williams was on third after a single when Banks slugged a three-run homer off Cards starter Jim "Mudcat" Grant. He doubled in the second, tripled home a run and scored on Ron Santo's homer in the fifth,

Billy Williams' flag still waves in the breeze high above Wrigley Field.

Commemorative button issued at Wrigley Field on Billy Williams Day in 1969.

and tripled home two runs in the sixth as the Cubs made it easy for Dick Selma, who pitched a complete-game four-hitter.

Williams had a single, a double, and two triples in his pocket when he came to bat in the eighth inning. He had hit for the cycle once in his career, and he was thinking about doing it again when he faced Cards reliever Dave Giusti.

"I went up there shooting for a home run," he said. "Naturally, I struck out. And I got a standing ovation. I don't know if anyone else ever got a sanding ovation for striking out. What a feeling that was."

Williams' consecutive-games streak stood as the NL record until 1983, when Steve Garvey of the Padres surpassed it. Williams is proud of the streak in that it symbolizes the durability and dependability that defined his career. It also embodies his work ethic and his approach to the game.

"I was just doing something I liked to do, playing baseball," he said. "And I was getting paid for it, so I felt I should be out there trying to help my team as much as I could."

The Cubs improved to 50–26 with the sweep. Anything seemed possible as they put 14$\frac{1}{2}$ games between themselves and the Cardinals in the NL East, while the upstart Mets were 8$\frac{1}{2}$ games back. The memory of a blissful June Sunday became

even more meaningful to Williams when the 1969 season unfolded as it did.

"I guess you'd have to say it was my day," he said. "We won a doubleheader and I got five hits. I felt like I had to repay the people who had been so nice to me, and I had done it. I felt like the luckiest man in the world."

After his retirement, Sweet-Swingin' Billy Williams wrote this autobiography for Triumph Books.

Billy Williams raises his cap to the Wrigley Field crowd on Billy Williams Day in 1969.

AUGUST 19, 1969: LUCKY KENNY HOLTZMAN AND HIS (FIRST) NO-HITTER

*Y*OU HAVE TO be lucky as hell to pitch a no-hitter; even the best hurlers know that. Kenny Holtzman was lucky his whole life.

I first learned about this pitcher's incredible luck in 1950-something when he was flipping baseball cards with me, the author of this book. We grew up together in University City, Missouri, a suburb of St. Louis. Kenny, my friend Herby Reznikoff, and I were flipping "for keeps" that day. Kenny walked away with all the cards.

A few years later, Kenny sat behind me in English class. I remember a surprise little quiz we had. He never studied much, but—as he said it—he was good at playing hunches—so he guessed at a lot of the answers. He got a huge *A* on his paper. I flunked it, big time.

His hunches, many expressed by shaking off his catchers' pitching signals years later, made him special at the mound. I went to see him at Wrigley in 1969 and asked Randy Huntley to tell him I was there. Huntley leaned out of the dugout after looking around and told me, "I forgot, Kenny has a 'reserve meeting' this weekend."

During that era, everyone who was in their twenties or thirties—that's most of the major leaguers of Kenny's era—knew all about reserve meetings. It was a place you went to—an armory, a naval yard, or an air field—in a military uniform, to serve your country. Military reservists of that era—affectionately called "weekend warriors"—were avoiding the military draft that was sending all the young men to Vietnam. Both Kenny and I were in the reserves—he in the army, I in the air force—and a lot of reserve units were activated in the late '60s and '70s and went to Southeast Asia. But not I, or Kenny either. As I said, he was lucky as hell!

My luck wasn't so great, though, during the 1969 season. I was working for the *Chicago Tribune*, and the "boys"—the guys I worked with there—were secretly playing hooky, going to the ballgame. We were advertising salesmen, so we were expected to be out of the office a lot. Boy, did I miss something at Wrigley that day! It was one of the true highlights of a season in which almost nothing but great stuff happened…at least for the first five months.

A crowd of 37,514 packed Wrigley Field on a Thursday afternoon, anticipating a pitchers' duel between Cubs lefty Ken Holtzman, an emerging star at 23, and Phil Niekro, the ace of the Braves staff at 30. In the first year of division play,

The greatest third baseman in the team's history became its radio voice too when Lou Boudreau left the broadcast booth to retire at WGN Radio.

RON SANTO was the premier third baseman of his time in the National League and was selected as an All-Star eight times. Five Gold Gloves were among his trophies, and he was clearly regarded as the finest fielder at his position in the National League. His career numbers include a robust 337 homers and 1,290 RBIs as a Cub.

He was a man who knew how to overcome adversity. He played his entire career with type 1 diabetes, formerly known as juvenile diabetes. In 1973 his mother and stepfather were killed in an automobile crash on their way to spring training. Through it all, he was always a man on a mission once he stepped across the white lines.

Santo's passion was never more evident than when he began jumping for joy and clicking his heels after Cubs wins in 1969. With the Cubs down a run in the ninth, Jim Hickman homered to win the game against the Cardinals, and Santo was in heaven. It started a tradition.

When Hickman came around, Santo exclaimed, "I went up in the air and I clicked my heels one time…I got home…I turned on WGN-TV to watch the highlights…. The next day I came into the clubhouse, and Leo [Durocher] came down to me and he said, 'Can you continue to click your heels?'" It never stopped. Santo's heels and the

trademark click became a symbol of the Cubs every time the third baseman saluted his team when they prevailed.

The joy of '69 faded painfully in September of that year, and the Cubs were unable to make any more progress in the next four seasons. In 1974 Santo was traded across town to the White Sox for three players, including pitcher Steve Stone. After a miserable season, which included a lengthy stint at second base, Santo retired. Bladder cancer finally claimed the Cub's life in 2010.

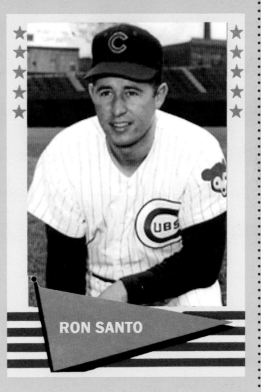

RON SANTO

RON SANTO
(1960–1974)

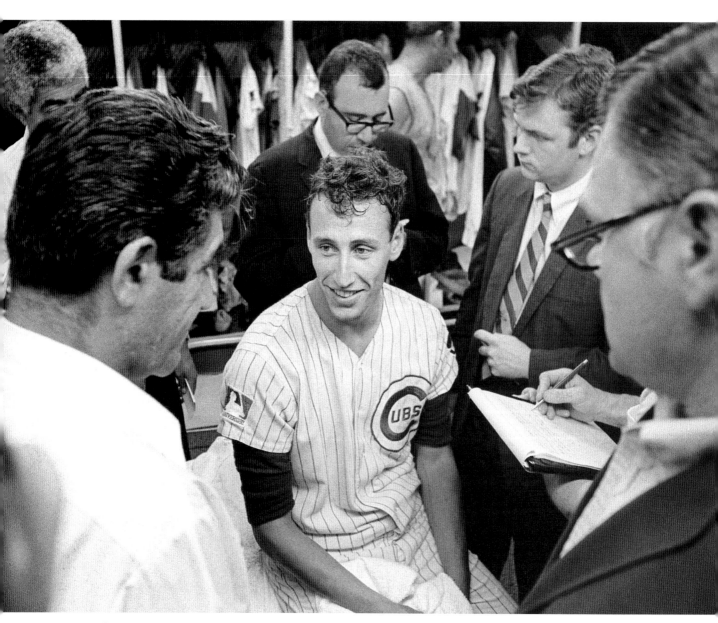

Cubs pitcher Ken Holtzman talks with newsmen in the clubhouse after his no-hitter against Atlanta in Chicago on August 19, 1969. The 23-year-old lefty, who issued three walks, used "90 percent fastballs" en route to his first no-hitter.

the Cubs were leading the NL East and the Braves were only 1¹/₂ games behind in the NL West, so the game had possible postseason implications as well.

Niekro got off to a shaky start, touched for singles by Don Kessinger and Glenn Beckert, the first two Cubs hitters. When Ron Santo reached the bleachers with a liner driven through the teeth of an incoming breeze, the Cubs had a 3–0 lead.

Niekro settled down and allowed only two singles thereafter. Holtzman, though, was overpowering, cruising through a formidable Atlanta lineup that featured Felipe Alou, Henry Aaron, Rico Carty, and Orlando Cepeda. The Braves were hitless through six innings.

That appeared to change when Aaron, leading off the seventh, snapped his wrists into a fastball and sent it soaring "toward Evanston," Holtzman recalled. "I thought it was gone for sure."

So did the crowd, based on the telltale *crack* of the bat. But left fielder Billy Williams never gave up on the ball. He drifted back into the "well area" where the left-field wall curved back into the outfield. The ball was hit nearly as high as it was far, and Williams was there to grab it when it hung up in the wind, then drifted back into the ballpark, as if pulled back on a string.

"Only the wind saved that ball from being a home run," Holtzman acknowledged, recalling the quizzical look Aaron gave him as he circled back to the dugout. "I thought it was going to land in those houses across the street." But I told you, he was *lucky!*

Given a reprieve, Holtzman retired eight of the next nine hitters, but a walk to Carty meant he had to face Aaron again, with two outs and nobody on in the ninth inning. Second baseman Beckert made a nice play on Aaron's sharply hit grounder, then appeared to stumble just a bit. "Throw it, kid," announcer Jack Brickhouse implored, and Beckert did, retiring Aaron for the final out.

"He did it! A no-hitter for Kenny Holtzman!" Brickhouse declared, and the celebration was on.

KEN HOLTZMAN
Pitcher

Chicago Cubs

This Ken Holtzman card had new meaning as a collectible after 1969. On August 19 of that year, he was a no-hitting pitcher and had one of the lowest ERAs in baseball.

PITCHING STATISTICS,
Atlanta Braves, Chicago Cubs, August 19, 1969

Atlanta Braves	IP	H	R	ER	BB	SO
Niekro L (16–11)	7.0	5	3	3	2	4
Neibauer	1.0	0	0	0	0	0
Totals	8.0	5	3	3	2	4

Chicago Cubs	IP	H	R	ER	BB	SO
Holtzman W (14–7)	9.0	0	0	0	3	0
Totals	9.0	0	0	0	3	0

IP: Innings Pitched, H: Hits, R: Runs, ER: Earned Runs, BB: Bases on Balls, SO: Strikeouts

Holtzman threw 112 pitches. As dominant as he was, he did not strike out a single batter, getting 15 of his 27 outs on fly balls, most of them harmless, as the Braves kept popping up his high, hard fastball. I'll say it again: this guy was lucky!

"Sure, things have to be in your favor to pitch a no-hitter," Cubs manager Leo Durocher said. "A couple of those line drives today, on another day they might have been base hits. But a no-hitter is a no-hitter. His fastball was really humming today."

The Cubs improved to a season-best 77–45 with the win and maintained their eight-game lead over the second-place Mets. It was their last hurrah. They would lose seven of their next nine games and 25 of their remaining 40. Holtzman was not immune to the slump, dropping six of his last nine decisions.

The lead would be gone in less than a month as the Mets went 33–11 after August 19 and won the division. Some Cubs fans still aren't over it.

Twenty years later I ran into one of the "boys" at the *Tribune* who illicitly took the day off to go to Wrigley that day. His name was Mario Tufano, a good Italian boy who always made it clear that he always wanted to make his mother proud.

"Do you know how it feels," Mario told me decades later, "to see a *no-hitter*, and you can't tell anyone what you saw that day? Not your mother!"

Always lucky, Holtzman had a second no-hitter for the Cubs on June 3, 1971, against the Cincinnati Reds—the first at Riverfront Stadium. Holtzman became the first Cubs pitcher since Larry Corcoran (who had three from 1880 to 1884) to have two no-hitters for the Cubs (though only one at Wrigley).

MAY 12, 1970: ERNIE BELTS NO. 500

SEVENTEEN YEARS BEFORE, on a sunny Sunday afternoon in St. Louis, a lanky 22-year-old shortstop named Ernie Banks had hit the first home run of his major league career, a drive to left field off 18-game-winner Gerry Staley.

Then, the same player, now age 39, was in the batter's box at Wrigley Field, facing Atlanta right-hander Pat Jarvis in the second inning and well aware that the next home run he hit would be the 500th of his career.

Ernie had to be thinking of all the things that had happened to him and all he had accomplished since that day in St. Louis. He had:

• hit five grand slams, a single-season record, in 1955;
• hit 40-plus homers in 1955, '57, '58, '59, and '60;
• won back-to-back MVP Awards in 1958 and '59;
• been named to the NL All-Star team 11 times;
• won the Gold Glove at shortstop in 1960;
• given Wrigley Field a second name, the Friendly Confines;
• become universally known as Mr. Cub;
• become beloved by a city's baseball fans, even those of the White Sox;

• taken to giving out annual "predictions" for the Cubs, such as, "The Cubs will arrive in '55," or "The Cubs will roar in '64."

His sunny disposition was evident from the first words he would utter upon stepping onto the field each day for pregame warm-ups: "Let's play two!" One of his teammates, reliever Phil Regan, said this:

"He is an inspiration to the older guys as well as the rookies. Sometimes we complain about the travel or the conditions or something, and then we see Ernie lifting everybody up. All he wants to do is go out there and play ball. What a man."

Quite obviously, then, Banks had his own cheering section in that third-base dugout, especially on that day in 1970. His teammates knew he was struggling. Indeed, ol' Ern was batting just .241 with two homers and 13 RBIs through 24 games.

Only 5,264 hardy souls made their way to Wrigley Field on May 12, 1970, but they saw one of the great moments in Cubs history as Ernie Banks became the first member of the franchise to hit 500 home runs.

Banks had finished the 1969 season with 497 homers, so the countdown to 500 was the topic of conversation throughout the winter. He also was transitioning to a part-time role with the Cubs and struggled with limited at-bats.

When the season started, the pressure intensified as he went almost

FERGUSON "FERGIE" JENKINS (1966–1973, 1982–1983)

Tall and athletic, FERGUSON JENKINS could have had his pick of sports. As a kid he played baseball, basketball, and hockey—excelling at each. He even spent two years with the Harlem Globetrotters.

Fortunately for Cubs fans, the 6'5" Canadian-born "Fergie" settled on baseball and was drafted by the Phillies straight out of high school. The Cubs acquired Jenkins in 1966 and promptly converted the right-handed relief pitcher into a starter. The rest is history.

In his Cubs debut he hit a home run and got a win in relief. As the Cubs' All-Star representative that year, he struck out six All-Stars in three innings, landing himself a place in the record books. He appeared in three more All-Star Games in his career.

During the next five years Jenkins won 20-plus games in each, making him one of the best pitchers in the game. In 1969 he had a league-leading 273 strikeouts. In 1971 his 2.77 ERA led him to 24 wins and the first Cy Young Award for a Cubs pitcher. It didn't hurt that he hit six home runs of his own that year.

Baseball is fickle, and after a down season in 1973 Jenkins was traded to the Texas Rangers. But he was back in 1982 and 1983 to finish his career with the Cubs.

With club records for strikeouts (2,038), games started (347), and home runs allowed (271) among his claims to fame, Fergie Jenkins will go down in history as the best pitcher ever to play for the Cubs. He was elected to the National Baseball Hall of Fame in 1991.

500 HOME RUN HITTERS

COURTESY OF PETE ROSE HIT KING MARKETING INC. / CAPITAL CARDS

©2009 AmericanMemorabilia.com

This special card depicts perhaps baseball's most exclusive club, "the 500 Club," reserved for the few who launched 500 or more out of the park.

three weeks before his first home run of the season. Number 498 came on April 25, a high fly ball that floated into the left-field bleachers against Houston off *Ball Four* author Jim Bouton. Fourteen days later, Ernie hit number 499 against the Reds and Don Gullett, a towering blast that landed on Waveland Avenue.

"It was exciting working up to that," Banks said. "I didn't think about it that much, but there was a lot of talk about it. People were pulling for me to do it. My daughter was getting a little irritated that it was taking so long. She said, 'Dad, hit the home run so we can get the media off of our backs.' I told her, 'All right, Jen, I'll get it over with.' That day, against the Braves, May 12, 1970, in the [second]

inning I hit the home run." Number 500 came off Atlanta's Pat Jarvis and was a signature Banks home run—a low line drive that sailed into the left-field bleachers and bounced back onto the field.

Mr. Cub's teammates shared in his joy and his relief. "Ernie was pretty happy running around the bases, knowing he got to that milestone," recalled Fergie Jenkins. "Back then, there were only a few hitters who had 500 home runs. It was a milestone for Ernie and for the Cubs. Everybody was pretty happy. The dugout was jumping around, patting everybody on the back, and happy for Ernie."

"I realized the impact of it and what it meant to people," Banks said. "Jack Brickhouse was there, and he was so

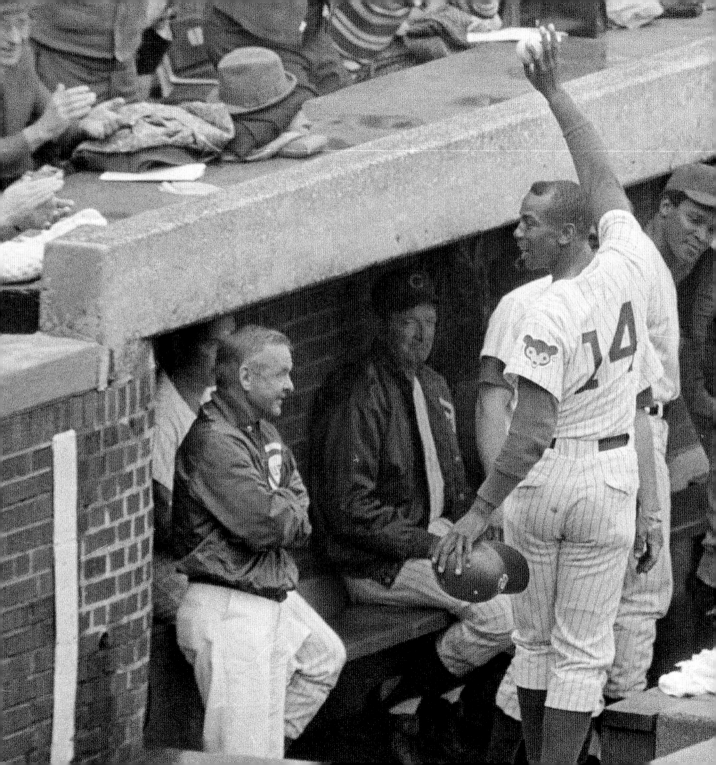

After hitting his 500th home run in the second inning of a game against the Atlanta Braves on May 12, 1970, Ernie Banks turns toward the Wrigley Field crowd to acknowledge their applause.

Ernie Banks' signed first-day cover, dated July 6, 1983.

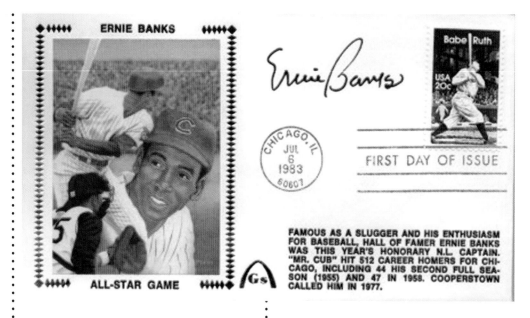

ERNIE BANKS

FIRST DAY OF ISSUE

FAMOUS AS A SLUGGER AND HIS ENTHUSIASM FOR BASEBALL, HALL OF FAMER ERNIE BANKS WAS THIS YEAR'S HONORARY N.L. CAPTAIN. "MR. CUB" HIT 512 CAREER HOMERS FOR CHICAGO, INCLUDING 44 HIS SECOND FULL SEASON (1955) AND 47 IN 1958. COOPERSTOWN CALLED HIM IN 1977.

ALL-STAR GAME

enthusiastic about it. I still play that tape and hear him saying, 'Oh, it's outta here. Wheeee, attaboy!' It kind of lifts up my spirits and all that. It's one thing I do when I get down, I play that Jack Brickhouse tape of my 500th home run. I was overjoyed by it. I went around the city and lots of places, and everyone was happy for me. I learned from that. Sports and the Cubs are just one thing that make people very happy, not just for a moment. People still come up and tell me, 'I was at that game.'"

The highlight quickly became one of the treasures of the WGN Sports vault, and sports editor Jack Rosenberg was delighted for Banks. "Ernie's first full year [1954] was the same as mine, so I always felt like we came up together," he said. "That was a big moment, one of the most highly anticipated home runs you will ever see."

At the time, Ernie was only the 10th member of the 500-home-run club. The solo shot also set a milestone as Banks reached 1,600 RBIs for his career. In a strange twist, ex-Cub Frank Secory was one of the umpires for the game. Secory also was working the game in 1953 when Banks hit his first home run. Reaching the milestone provided a brief glimpse of sunlight following the dark days at the end of 1969 and gave fans the satisfaction of seeing the great Cubs player join one of baseball's most exclusive clubs.

SEPTEMBER 2, 1972: ALMOST PERFECT—MILT PAPPAS' "DISAPPOINTING NO-HITTER"

A "DISAPPOINTING NO-HITTER" sounds like the greatest baseball oxymoron of all time, but Milt Pappas' 1972 gem against the San Diego Padres has come to be known as exactly that. On September 2, after the Cubs opened up an 8–0 lead, all eyes turned to Pappas, who went to the ninth inning with a perfect game on the line.

"A pitcher is aware of what's going on, and by the time you get to the seventh or eighth inning, the bench knows what is going on," said Pappas. "That day, when I came in after the eighth inning and I still had the perfect game, I walked down the bench and no one said a word. That was ridiculous, and I wanted my guys to get going, so I said, 'Hey guys, I'm throwing a no-hitter,' and that got them loose and were laughing. Then I got tight because where I was sitting in the dugout, the cops and ushers were gathering and making a racket, so I had to ask them to be quiet."

The ninth inning opened with a routine fly to center field off the bat of John Jeter, but Cubs center fielder Bill North slipped when his feet went out from under him, and it looked like the perfect game might fall with him. From out of nowhere, Billy Williams raced in, hat flying off, and reached out to grab the ball for the first out. "When I saw Billy North slip down, my heart sank down to my toes, and I thought, *There goes everything*," said Pappas. "Thankfully, Billy was hustling."

Williams never took anything for granted as a player, especially with history on the line. "As I was drifting over I could

There was hardly a Greek kid in Chicago who didn't have this baseball card among his collection.

MILT
PAPPAS
CHICAGO CUBS

PITCHER

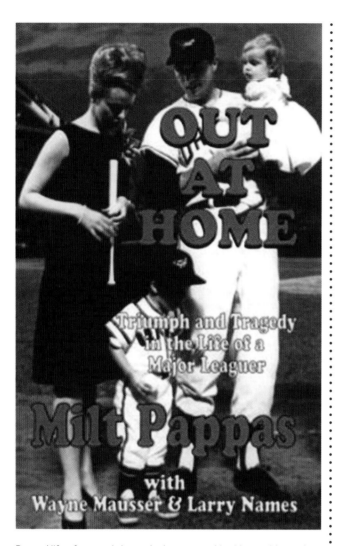

Pappas' life of ups and downs is documented in this autobiography. It includes baseball heroics; a "perfect game" (of which many say he was robbed); and the disappearance of his wife, who was later found dead, possibly murdered in a satanic ritual.

see him, and all of a sudden I had to come in and make a shoestring catch to catch the ball," he said. Moments later, Fred Kendall (Jason's father) ripped a drive to left that was barely foul, then grounded to Don Kessinger at short for the second out.

The Padres sent up Larry Stahl to pinch-hit with the perfect game on the line, and Pappas quickly got ahead 1–2. After having everything go his way throughout the game, fortune (and the home-plate umpire, Bruce Froemming) deserted him at the last minute.

"I'm one pitch from the greatest thing a pitcher can do," he said. "Next pitch was a slider on the outside corner, ball two. Next pitch, another slider on the corner, ball three. All these pitches were right there, and I'm saying, 'C'mon, Froemming, they're all right there.' Now comes the 3–2 pitch, again on the outside corner, ball four. I went crazy. I called Bruce Froemming every name you can think of. I knew he didn't have the guts to throw me out because I still had the no-hitter. The next guy, Garry Jestadt popped up to Carmen Fanzone, and I got the no-hitter, which was great. But those balls should have been called strikes." Randy Hundley was behind the plate for his second no-hitter of the year. (Burt Hooton had thrown one in April.)

"That was a little disappointing in that we didn't get the perfect game," said Hundley. "There were a couple of pitches that were questionable, but I think if Bruce Froemming had called those pitches, nobody would have ever said a word about it. We ended up walking one hitter and the next hitter pops up and we get the no-hitter. It would have been wonderful to have had a perfect game. We probably wouldn't be talking about it [at this time] if we had a perfect game."

The Cubs catcher still marvels at Pappas' pinpoint control that day. "One of the things about Milt was he hardly ever shook me off," Hundley said. "I would go down with the sign, and he would come with the pitch right away. The same thing happened this day. He only had a fastball and slider to work with. It was frustrating at times to get hitters out with just two pitches, but I'm telling you, I could sit there and close my eyes, and he could hit that mitt. It was just unbelievable how he did and what great control he had that day."

In the *Chicago Tribune* the next day, Pappas talked about understanding the close pitches, but the years have hardened his stance. "When you look at the last pitch to Dale Mitchell in Don Larsen's perfect game, it's not even close, but there was a perfect game on the line. The thing that got me was that smirk on Froemming's face after the pitch. The next day, he actually asked me to sign a baseball, and I said, 'I would be more than happy to, Bruce, and you know where you can stick it.'"

Fergie Jenkins never threw a no-hitter in his career but was excited to see another teammate join that exclusive club. "I was on the bench charting the game," he said. "Milt to this day said Bruce Froemming should have called it a strike, but, hey, the umpire is going to call his game. He pitched a no-hitter, but not a perfect game. Not bad."

Rick Monday was with the Cubs at the time, but he wants no part of the controversy. "I was at a banquet one night with Bruce, and he was asked by someone in the audience, 'You know, you were the umpire behind home plate when Pappas had the no-hitter going. There were two outs in the top of the ninth, and you called ball four. Did you know you had a chance to become only the 13th umpire to ever call a perfect game in major league history?' Bruce looked at the guy and said, 'Was it really that important?' and the guy said, 'Oh yeah.' And Bruce said, 'Name the other 12 home-plate umpires during the perfect games.'

"And that is Bruce's take. Don't get in between them. If you are invited to the same dinner party, you might want to stay a little bit farther away from them.

Cubs pitcher Milt Pappas humbly relates his feelings to newsmen after he pitched his 200th career win against the Montreal Expos at Wrigley Field on September 21, 1972.

Was the pitch outside? Two guys had really good looks at it, and they both differ in their opinions."

"That was the only time I ever pitched a no-hitter in all my years of Babe Ruth, high school, minor leagues, anything," said Pappas. His gem ended a run of four Cubs no-hitters in four seasons (Holtzman 1969, Holtzman 1971, and Hooton 1972) and is the last no-no thrown by a Cubs pitcher. Pappas is the only man in major league history to lose a perfect game with one out to go and complete a no-hitter by retiring the next batter. He is also the only pitcher to lose a perfect game by walking the 27th batter.

PART V

1980s and 1990s

In 1982 Harry Caray began the tradition of crooning "Take Me Out to the Ball Game" during the seventh-inning stretch; by '88 Wrigley Field had lights, and by 1998 Wrigley Field—thanks to Sammy Sosa—became the center of attention for baseball fans everywhere, except those in Mark McGwire's family in St. Louis.

1982: HARRY CARAY STARTS A SINGING TRADITION

HARRY CARAY AND "Take Me Out to the Ballgame" both endured long, successful careers before they became a duet in the Wrigley Field broadcast booth. The story, however, goes back, way back. Ah-one, ah-two, ah-three…

"Take Me Out to the Ballgame" was written by Jack Norworth and Albert Von Tilzer in 1908. That year's desperate pennant races turned the tune into a hit as the Cubs rallied to win the World Series. It was to be the Cubs' last title for more than a century, but the team reclaimed the song when Harry Caray moved across town in 1982.

Caray had already spent 36 years as a major league broadcaster, mostly with the Cardinals (1945–69) and White Sox (1971–81), plus a year with cantankerous Oakland A's owner Charlie Finley. It was with the White Sox that Caray's private singing of "Take Me Out to the Ballgame" became public when owner Bill Veeck had a microphone secretly turned on during one seventh-inning stretch. After new management took over the Sox, Caray headed for the North Side.

The Wrigley home opener on April 9, 1982, marked Fergie Jenkins' return after eight seasons in exile, but that game is more memorable in Cubs annals as Harry

Chicago Cubs broadcaster Harry Caray leads Mayor Richard M. Daley in a rendition of "Take Me Out to the Ball Game" on August 26, 1989, outside Caray's namesake restaurant.

Caray's debut at the Friendly Confines. "All right, let me hear ya!" Hear him they did.

Though it was frigid, 27,000 joined in as Caray extorted them to "root, root, root for the Cubbies." He then turned around his microphone for them to call out the strikes at the old ballgame. The Cubs won, and the former "Voice of the Sox" had won over the Cubs crowd.

North Siders who'd considered Caray a clown during his decade at Comiskey Park quickly fell for St. Louis–born Harry Christopher Carabina. A first-generation American of Romanian, French, and Italian descent, he was a basketball backboard salesman whose start in broadcasting came after telling KMOX their Cardinals announcers were "as dull and boring as the morning crop reports."

Caray had been going by his alias for decades by the time he arrived at Wrigley. At 63, he was the exuberant, irreverent grandfather in wide-rimmed glasses regaling anyone who'd listen to his tales old and new. It wasn't merely acceptable to put work, school, and chores aside in the middle of the day to follow the Cubs, Caray told everyone that there was no better place on earth to be than Wrigley. Caray said, "My whole philosophy is to broadcast the way a fan would broadcast." The fans followed.

As the Cubs battled for their first postseason appearance in 39 years in 1984, attendance at Wrigley hit two million for the first time. WGN-TV, upgraded to a "superstation" in the burgeoning cable market, could then be seen all over the country. Even after Wrigley got lights in 1988, the Cubs remained prime daytime programming. Harry Caray was national.

"Cub fan, Bud man," proclaimed banners and commercials with a dancing Harry dressed like a long-lost Blues Brother; never mind that he'd been fired by the owners of the brewery—and the Cardinals—in 1969. Caray didn't just make appearances at bars and restaurants, he had his own chain. And he was responsible for three generations of baseball announcers with son Skip and grandson, Chip. "Holy Cow!"

Even after suffering a stroke in 1987, the 68-year-old Harry was soon back in the booth, mangling names and calling plays in his own unique style. "Cubs win! What a lucky break! The good Lord wants the Cubs to win!" Caray died of a heart attack at age 78 in February 1998, preparing for a new season.

Caray helped turn the Cubs into a phenomenon. Those who only know his statue outside Wrigley can still hear him at every Cubs home game as special guests (starting with actor and Cubs fan Bill Murray) sing Norworth and Von Tilzer's—oh, who are we kidding, it's Harry Caray's song. "Now let's get some runs."

"Voice of the Cubs" Harry Caray sings "Take Me Out to the Ball Game" during the seventh-inning stretch from the WGN broadcast booth, a tradition he started in 1982 and that lives on today.

AUGUST 18, 1982: TURNING 21 AT WRIGLEY

THE SUMMER OF 1982 was not a successful one for the 73–89 Cubs, but the season had its share of memorable games. There was the two-and-a-half-hour rally on July 16, which started with a 10th-inning single by Junior Kennedy and culminated with a Jay Johnstone game-winning hit after more than 120 minutes of waiting out the rain. There was the here-today-gone-today saga of Joel Youngblood, who banged out a two-run hit as a Met at Wrigley on the afternoon of August 4 and then singled as an Expo that night in Philadelphia after being traded—the only player with two hits in two cities in two uniforms in one day. And then there was the game without end.

When you play in a ballpark without lights, there are bound to be games that simply require more time than there are hours in the day—or daylight. Such was the case when the Cubs opened a series with the Dodgers at Wrigley Field on Tuesday, August 17. It started for the Cubs with Ryne Sandberg leading off with a single, stealing second, being sacrificed to third, and scoring on Bill Buckner's groundout. You could say playing for one run was prudent, but you could also argue that manager Lee Elia should have had

Dickie Noles pitch around Mike Scioscia the next inning with a man on second, two out, and pitcher Burt Hooton on deck. Instead, Scioscia singled home Bill Russell. There would be plenty of time for second-guessing.

After 17 innings, with the score still tied 1–1, the game was suspended because of darkness. The teams were required to finish this business Wednesday before commencing their regularly scheduled game. And day two got weird. Umpire Dave Pallone ejected Dodger Ron Cey after he was picked off by Allen Ripley in the 20th. Manager Tommy Lasorda claimed the ejection of the "Penguin" was a deliberate attempt to get the Dodgers to forfeit and finally end the game; the conspiracy theory got Lasorda ejected too. Elia had been thrown out the day before.

With Pedro Guerrero moving from right field to third base, pitcher Fernando Valenzuela took over in right and hauled in a fly ball before being swapping corner positions with Dusty Baker because a lefty was coming up against Jerry Reuss, the day's scheduled starting pitcher, who, like everyone else, was handling extra duty. The Dodgers pushed across a run in the 21st when Baker lifted a fly to right. Umpire Eric Gregg first called Steve Sax out at the plate—then said to himself, "What am I doing?" He ruled Sax safe.

The 25th and final man on the Dodgers bench, pitcher Bob Welch, went to the outfield in Valenzuela's place in the bottom of the 22nd. For defense, apparently. Reuss retired the side in order to earn the win and then picked up another *W* with five innings in the regularly scheduled game—the 7–4 Dodgers win mercifully ended in nine innings and in a tidy two hours, 21 minutes. The first game that day had been the longest game ever at Wrigley in terms of time (6:10) and innings (21). As if by way of restitution from the baseball gods, the Cubs did not play another extra-inning game in 1982 and escaped the basement for good after winning the finale of that grueling Dodgers series.

Perhaps Lee Elia couldn't help but revisit the two-day, 21-inning affair when the Dodgers came to town the following April. A 4–3 loss to L.A. sent the manager on one of the most famous profanity-filled tirades in the history of bleeped audio. "You're stuck in a —— stigma of the —— Dodgers and the Phillies and the Cardinals and all that cheap —— It's unbelievable. It really is." It's unbelievable that just a year later, after Elia was let go, those hard-working Cubs were the toast of Chicago. —— unbelievable.

Umpire Ed Vargo, right, tries to break up a heated argument between Cubs manager Lee Elia, center, and home-plate umpire Eric Gregg after a disputed call during the eighth inning of the August 17, 1982, Cubs-Dodgers game at Wrigley.

THE HECKLER

Chicagoland teens too busy playing Pac-Man to follow Cubs' playoff run

Stupid White Sox manager Tony La Russa never to amount to anything!

VOL. MXLVI   THURSDAY, OCTOBER 4, 1984   No. 378

Cubs Head to San Diego Poised for NLCS Sweep

Slick-fielding 1B Durham leads Chicago as Padres 'total jerk' Steve Garvey sure to choke

The Cubs clubhouse was all smiles Wednesday night as they headed to sunny San Diego where they planned to close out the down-and-out San Diego Padres in a three-game sweep of the N. L. Championship Series.

A highlight of the Cubs run to the title has been the outstanding glove work of 1B Leon Durham who's had only seven errors all season. "I've always taken pride in my fielding," said Durham, who gobbles

up every ball that comes his way. "My secret is to spill a little Gatorade on my glove before every inning."

Here's hoping the Gatorade keeps flowing as Durham's sure hands lead the Cubs to the pennant.

OTHER NEWS FROM THE CUBS' ROAD TO A WORLD SERIES TITLE

- Newfangled 'Macintosh' computer predicts Cubs win World Series against Tigers in 5
- Padres' Gwynn starting to look a little tubby
- Closer Lee Smith declares Garvey's arms 'too short' to hit home runs
- Ryne Sandberg ready for any bad hop that comes his way
- Mananger Frey, coach Zimmer emphasize team hydration with new Gatorade cooler
- Fan who says woo all the time growing 'kind of annoying' to Cubs fans, players and neighbors in 10-block radius of Wrigley Field
- Staff ace Sutcliffe giving hope to red-headed step-children everywhere
- Fans outraged by scalpers' demands for $6 front row tickets
- Harry Caray looks forward to World Series celebration, alcohol poisoning

Durham prepares to haul in another routine grounder like so many others this season.

The headline was encouraging, but it didn't happen. The Cubs blew it and "next year" was—as always—on everyone's mind by the close of postseason play.

1984: SECOND CITY PANDEMONIUM, ORWELLIAN CLIMAX

*I*N THE 38 seasons between their last pennant in 1945 and their dismal 1983 finish, the Cubs finished last or next-to-last 20 times. They did so in every format: an eight-team league (until 1961), a 10-team league (1962–68), and a six-team division (1969–83). "No matter how you slice it," as a candy bar commercial of the day said, "it comes up peanuts." And being a Cubs fan could make a person nuts.

General manager Dallas Green's choice to manage the Cubs in 1984 was Jim Frey, whose Royals had gone up

against Green's Phillies—and lost—in the 1980 World Series. Yet the Phillies would be the losers when Green was hired by the new owners, the Tribune Company, after the 1981 season. Green hijacked Keith Moreland and Ryne Sandberg from his old organization that winter and snagged Gary Matthews and Bob Dernier from the Phillies in spring training of 1984. After shaking off the rust that had seen the Cubs go 7–20 in spring training and release beloved-but-aged Fergie Jenkins, Chicago bloomed in 1984—the year George Orwell had warned us about.

The Cubs won eight of nine games heading into Memorial Day weekend to reach 11 games over .500—heights not seen at Wrigley Field in five years. Having found more than enough offense via Philadelphia, Green filled his pitching needs from the American League: Dennis Eckersley from Boston (for Bill Buckner) and Rick Sutcliffe from Cleveland (in a six-player deal that shipped out Joe Carter and Mel Hall). Yet after the deadline deal for Sutcliffe in mid-June, the Cubs fell out of first place, supplanted by the Mets. Not only did the Mets hail from loathed New York, they had spoiled Chicago's best chance at a pennant in the past four decades, in 1969. Players and management had changed on both sides, but the fans had not forgotten.

Ryne Sandberg is greeted by ecstatic fans after the Cubs clinched the National League East pennant by beating the Pirates in Pittsburgh on September 24, 1984.

The National League East turned upside down in 1984. The Cubs and Mets, who had spent the last five years fighting over last place, now battled it out for first. As July wound down, the Mets held a four-and-a-half-game edge, but the Cubs, famous for their summer swoons, won three of four in New York and then swept four straight at Wrigley, amid brawls between Mets players and Cubs fans. Chicago exorcised past ghosts, winning 12 of 18 against the Mets and going 13–5 against the defending world-champion Cardinals, the most memorable coming in an NBC *Game of the Week* when Sandberg, NL MVP-to-be, twice hit game-tying home runs off ex-Cub and Cy Young–winner Bruce Sutter in a 12-inning win remembered simply as "the Sandberg Game."

The Cubs clinched in Pittsburgh on September 24 with Sutcliffe's 20th win of the year—his 16–1 mark as a Cub

Sports Illustrated portrayed him as the Cubs' superstar, but Leon "Bull" Durham was largely disregarded after an easy ground ball went through his legs, causing the Cubs to give away the NLCS title to the Padres.

Budding Superstar
Bull Durham

Harry Caray's following was so big that it was he—not a Cub, a manager, or a coach—who was featured on the program of the NLDS.

earning him the National League Cy Young Award despite having spent two-plus months in the American League. On the final day of the season, after setting a then–Wrigley attendance record of 2.1 million, the Cubs beat Sutter again with a late rally for their 96th win. The fans would not leave, cheering long and loud until the players reappeared on the field in shower shoes and sweatshirts. Curtain calls just weren't done then, but neither were Cubs playoff teams. This was special.

The first Cubs postseason game in a generation—make that two generations—became another celebration. Bob Dernier homered in the first postseason at-bat by a Cub since 1945, and "Sarge"—Gary Matthews—drilled another ball into the outgoing breeze two batters later. Sutcliffe, of course, started on the mound, but his bat kicked the party into high gear. He led off the third with a home run as the fans went even crazier on the summerlike October afternoon.

The lone Padres rally was snuffed in the fourth when a soft fly with the bases loaded was carried by the wind into the glove of diving Keith Moreland. An inning later, Sarge slammed a three-run home run. Ron Cey added a homer an inning after that. The 13–0 drubbing saw every Cub collect at least one hit and one run batted in. It was not outrageous to think back

The Rick Sutcliffe deal is recalled when it comes to 1984 Cubs in-season acquisitions. A deal a few weeks earlier for DENNIS ECKERSLEY, however, set the stage for a beefed-up rotation that helped end a four-decade postseason drought.

Though 10 games over .500 in late May, the Cubs were down two starters due to injuries. So general manager Dallas Green shipped Bill Buckner to Boston for Eckersley and infielder Mike Brumley. Eck, 29, with a career mark of 124–102 and 3.69 ERA in 278 American League starts to that point, had a less than stellar National League debut. The Cubs lost six of his first seven starts as Eckersley pitched to a 5.57 ERA. Come July, however, everything turned around.

The Cubs won 12 of his last 17 starts— Eck was 9–3 with a 2.13 ERA down the stretch. Combined with Sutcliffe's 16–1 mark in just more than half a season, the Cubs rallied from four and a half games back to reach the postseason for the first time since 1945. Eckersley was hit hard in his lone NLCS start, but one can't help wonder what might have been if manager Jim Frey had summoned Eck in relief in Game 5 in San Diego. He pitched just once in relief in three seasons in Chicago before becoming a legendary reliever with the A's. An abysmal 1986 season resulted in the Cubs trading him for three players who never left the minors. Eckersley was traded to his native Oakland at the end of camp in 1987.

A dozen seasons and 387 saves later (he began his career with three saves for Cleveland), Eck was a Hall of Famer.

Cy Young and MVP winner in 1992, he spent all but one year post-Cubs with manager Tony La Russa and pitching coach Dave Duncan in Oakland and St. Louis. The only pitcher with 100 complete games and 300 saves, Eck certainly was one of a kind.

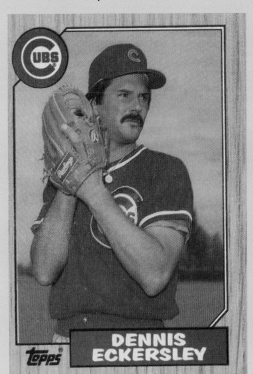

With Eckersley's ample awards and honors, this Topps baseball card was a must for every Cubs fan who collected cards.

DENNIS ECKERSLEY
(1984–1986)

to the 1945 World Series and visualize a rematch against the Tigers, the 1984 AL East champs.

The only wind in Game 2 came from the Cubs whirling around the bases like something from the Tinker-Evers-Chance days: going first to third on an infield out, taking the extra base on a throw past the cutoff man, a stolen base at a key moment, and a clutch two-out hit. Steve Trout was masterful, pitching into the ninth before Lee Smith nailed down the 4–2 win. Team executives were already quibbling with the network about World Series start times—Wrigley's lack of lights would alter the home-field-advantage rotation. NBC would not consider weekday afternoon World Series games. This was not 1945.

It was San Diego's first-ever postseason, and Jack Murphy Stadium was jumping for Game 3 as Ed Whitson pitched out of early trouble. Dennis Eckersley could wriggle out of only so many jams before the Padres scored more times in the fifth than they had in their first 22 playoff innings. A three-run shot by Kevin McReynolds off George Frazier capped a 7–1 Padres win.

Game 4 belonged to Steve Garvey. Dallas Green had tried to sign the first baseman in 1983; the Padres outbid the Cubs, but Garvey still made Chicago pay. After flying out his first time up against Scott Sanderson, Garvey produced run-scoring hits in his next four at-bats, negating game-tying hits by Jody Davis in the fourth and the eighth. After homering just eight times all season, Garvey launched a two-run shot off Lee Smith to force a deciding game.

Game 5 seemed to follow some long-ago-written tragic formula: the unbeatable star pitcher on the mound, a 3–0 lead, and one win needed to reach the World Series. Leon Durham, who gave the Cubs the lead with a two-run homer in the first inning, had his name written in the cannon of dishonor when a grounder went through his legs to bring in the tying run in the seventh. Tony Gwynn's two-run double gave the Padres the lead and Garvey wrapped up the series—and series MVP—with his seventh RBI.

Chicago's autumn was ruined, its long winter occupied by the idea that starting in 1985, the NLCS would become a best-of-seven. This would have given the Cubs two extra home games if only the format had begun a year earlier. As Orwell penned in *1984*, "Progress in our world will be progress toward more pain."

A native of Spokane, Washington, RYNE SANDBERG was named to *Parade* magazine's High School All-America football team and was later recruited to play quarterback at Washington State University. But his calling was baseball. By 1978 he was drafted by the Phillies in the 20th round as one of their farm club infielders. By 1981 he was the Phillies shortstop.

Traded to the Cubs in 1982, he was a solid rookie who took his game to new heights in 1984, easily winning the National League Most Valuable Player Award with a dream season in 1984 (.314, 36 doubles, 19 triples, 19 homers, 84 RBIs, 32 steals, and a league-leading 114 runs scored), launching a decade of dominance as the preeminent second baseman in baseball.

One of the most popular players on the Cubs, he led his young club to an NL East crown in 1989 but was denied a spot in the World Series by the San Francisco Giants. In 1990 Sandberg had his best statistical year when he hit 40 home runs and drove in 100, while stealing 25 bases. More than just a star player, "Ryno" was beloved by Cubs fans for being the personification of a true ball-player—hardworking, team-first, never flashy, but always steady.

The 10-time All-Star won nine Gold Gloves and set a major league record for career fielding percentage by a second baseman (.989). Sandberg's abrupt retirement came as a shock in 1994, but his return to the game in 1996–97 did not, and neither did his endless enthusiasm, smooth stroke, or ability to flag down almost anything hit to the right side of the infield.

RYNE SANDBERG (1982–1994, 1996–1997)

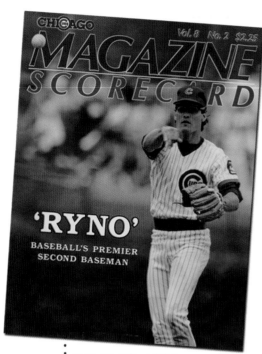

The *Scorecard* identified Ryne Sandberg as the game's best second baseman, but it neglected to point out he may have been the favorite Cub of his era.

JUNE 23, 1984: THE SANDBERG GAME

*C*AN ONE GAME be credited with launching an MVP season? A Hall of Fame career? A franchise turnaround? In the case of Ryne Sandberg vs. the St. Louis Cardinals on a warm June Saturday in 1984, the answer to all three questions is yes. It was that kind of game.

Wrigley Field was packed with 38,079 spectators. Bob Costas and Tony Kubek were in the house for NBC's national *Game of the Week* telecast. The speedy Cardinals were not only the Cubs'

archrivals, they were one of the dominant teams in baseball, in the midst of winning three pennants in six years.

St. Louis' Willie McGee hit for the cycle and drove in six runs. Ozzie Smith was 2-for-4 and scored four times; Tommy Herr was 3-for-6. When the Cards entrusted a 9–8 lead to Bruce Sutter—the Hall of Fame reliever who had won the Cy Young Award for the Cubs five years earlier and was on his way to a career-best 45 saves—it looked like *game over*.

Enter Sandberg. Leading off the bottom of the ninth, he caught a split-finger pitch from Sutter that didn't dive as sharply as Sutter's signature splitter typically did, and he drove it into the bleachers in left-center field for a game-tying home run.

The crowd erupted…and McGee countered. Facing Lee Smith, the Cubs' All-Star closer, with Ozzie Smith at second and nobody out in the 10th, McGee lined a double to right field, scoring Ozzie Smith with the go-ahead run. McGee came around on two groundouts, and the Cardinals led 11–9.

Sutter retired the first two Cubs in the 10th, then walked Bob Dernier, who got a favorable call when he checked his swing on Sutter's 3–2 pitch. That brought Sandberg to the plate, and he did it again, jumping on another hanging splitter and

driving it out of the ballpark for another game-tying homer.

"Do you believe it?" Costas asked the TV audience.

"He did it again!" Cubs broadcaster Harry Caray bellowed. "He did it again!"

The crowd summoned the reluctant Sandberg from the dugout for a curtain call, and they were still buzzing an inning later when Leon Durham led off the Cubs' 11th with a walk. He stole second and moved to third on catcher Darrell Porter's throwing error. After the Cardinals loaded the bases with two intentional walks, pinch hitter Dave Owen delivered a game-winning single. Owen was the Cubs' last available position player.

Ryne Sandberg glares back at home-plate umpire Larry Vanover following a called third strike in the second inning against the Pittsburgh Pirates on April 27, 1997, at Wrigley.

"That game kind of put me on the map," Sandberg said with characteristic understatement. "It wasn't much to [Sutter's] career, but it was everything to mine."

Cardinals manager Whitey Herzog had a stronger reaction. "I always thought Babe Ruth was the greatest player in baseball," Herzog said. "Now I'm not so sure."

Sandberg and McGee combined to go 9-for-12 with five runs scored and 13 RBIs. McGee's bases-loaded triple was the big hit in a six-run second inning that chased Cubs starter Steve Trout and gave the Cardinals a 7–1 lead. He hit a two-run homer in the sixth, putting the Cards ahead 9–3, and finished his 4-for-6, six-RBI day with that run-scoring double in the 10th.

Sandberg singled in a run in the Cubs' first and had an RBI groundout in the fifth. His two-run single in the sixth capped a five-run uprising that brought the Cubs within 9–8, putting him in position to go to work against Sutter.

Sandberg finished 5-for-6 with seven RBIs. Dernier was 3-for-5 and scored four runs. The Cubs got seven innings of scoreless relief from Rich Bordi, Warren Brusstar, Tim Stoddard, and George Frazier.

Sandberg didn't exactly "own" Sutter—he'd been 2-for-12 against him before this game. This genesis of his performance may have occurred in spring training. Jim Frey, the Cubs' first-year manager and an accomplished hitting coach, took note of Sandberg's size and strength and offered a suggestion.

"I told him, 'I know you're a team player, Ryno, and here's one thing you can do to help the team. You're a big, strong guy, and when you get a pitcher 2–0 or 3–1, you look for that fastball and pop it onto Waveland Avenue.'"

Sandberg totaled 15 homers in his first two big-league seasons. Taking Frey's suggestion to heart, he hit 19 in '84, along with 36 doubles and 19 triples. He batted .314, drove in 84 runs, scored a league-best 114 runs, stole 32 bases, and won a Gold Glove for fielding excellence. He was the runaway winner of the National League MVP Award as the Cubs reached the postseason for the first time since 1945…and all agree it all began on a warm afternoon in June.

"After baseball got so home-run happy I heard some people say, 'What's the big deal about two home runs in a game?'" Sandberg said. "National TV, the Cardinals, the circumstances, Bruce Sutter, who threw nothing but ground balls and was a lights-out closer…I guess it was a pretty big deal. I was amazed myself."

ANDRE DAWSON's decision to come to Chicago had little to do with the team or the money; it had to do with the grass. The 30-year-old outfielder's aching knees could not take another season on Montreal's turf. Dawson, in the prime of a Hall of Fame career, should have been able to write his ticket anywhere, but with major league owners secretly colluding to keep down free-agent salaries in the mid-1980s, Dawson seemed resigned to returning to the Expos, turf and all. "The Hawk" made a bold move, offering to leave the amount blank if the Cubs offered him a contract. General manager Dallas Green wrote in $500,000 (plus bonuses of $200,000 more). Dawson signed. It was one of the greatest deals in franchise history.

LAST SHALL BE FIRST—FOR MVP

While a dozen Cubs were paid more in 1987, no National League hitter did more than Dawson. He collected an NL-best 49 home runs, 137 RBIs, and 353 total bases. The Cubs were playing .500 ball into September, before a managerial change saw them fall into the basement (their 76 wins were still half a dozen more than in '86). Dawson became the first Most Valuable Player ever from a last-place team.

COOPERSTOWN CUB SNUB

Dawson was an All-Star five times as a Cub—starting four times—and earned the last two of his eight Gold Gloves. Though injured in 1989, seven of his 21 homers came in the final month as the Cubs took the NL East. After that first bargain year, Dawson received $12 million over his final five Chicago seasons. He moved on to the Red Sox (for a chance to be a designated hitter), and the Marlins (his hometown of Miami). The first 400-homer, 300-steal slugger besides Willie Mays, Dawson went into the Hall of Fame in 2010 as an Expo (Cooperstown's decision), but it was backing up his blank Cubs contract that got him there.

ANDRE DAWSON
(1987–1992)

The lights may have been new in 1988, but they had been sitting around the ballpark for more than 45 years. Originally they were scheduled to be installed in the 1940s, but the Japanese attack on Pearl Harbor in 1941 prompted fears that they might attract more Japanese bombers than Cubs fans.

AUGUST 8, 1988: LET THERE BE LIGHTS!

FOR ALL THE hoopla that accompanied the first night game at Wrigley Field—Cubs vs. Phillies on Monday, August 8, 1988—there was reason to wonder if the baseball gods endorsed the idea. Maybe it was the "8/8/88" implication of the date.

In any case, not long after 91-year-old Cubs fan Harry Grossman and retired Hall of Fame broadcaster Jack Brickhouse

flipped the switch to engage Wrigley's new lighting system, a rainstorm of biblical severity descended on the ballpark, drenching the place.

Ryne Sandberg had hit a home run, and the Cubs led 3–1 after three and a half innings. The umpires did not want to deprive the SRO crowd of their place in history, so they waited for a letup. But when rain was still falling heavily after two hours, they had no choice and called the game. Greg Maddux, Jody Davis, and Les Lancaster flopping around on the tarp that covered the field during the delay turned

out to be the evening's entertainment highlight.

The Mets were in the house the following night for the first "official" night game. The hoopla meter was turned way down, the weather cooperated, and the teams played baseball, with Sid Fernandez opposing Mike Bielecki.

Lenny Dykstra's two-run homer staked the Mets to a 2–0 lead in the fifth inning. The Cubs got on the board with Rafael Palmeiro's RBI triple in the fifth and squared it in the sixth when Shawon Dunston singled, stole second, and came around on two groundouts.

They won it with a four-spot in the seventh, chasing Fernandez when Jody Davis pinch-hit for Bielecki and stroked a double to left-center to score Palmeiro, who had singled. Roger McDowell relieved, and the Cubs peppered him with consecutive two-out singles by Dunston,

The lights are on at Wrigley!

Sandberg, Mark Grace, and Andre Dawson, building a 6–2 lead.

Howard Johnson homered in the Mets' eighth, and they got within 6–4 in the ninth when Gary Carter doubled and Dave Magadan singled him home. But Goose Gossage retired Tim Teufel, Lee Mazzilli, and Dykstra to save it for Frank DiPino, who earned the win with two innings of scoreless relief.

The Cubs' agreement with the city allowed them six night games in 1984. They went 3–3 in them. It was obvious to all who were there for any of them that night baseball was here to stay on the North Side.

A night game at Wrigley—an impossible feat before 1988.

1989 CHICAGO CUBS. 1989
NATIONAL LEAGUE EASTERN DIVISION CHAMPIONS
SEASON RECORD: WON 93 LOST 69

Ahhhh! How good that plaque looked and how well the Cubbies played in '89, but they didn't make it to the World Series... again.

1989: ZIM'S 89er RUSH

FOR THE SECOND time in five years, a Cubs team that had previously showed a disinclination toward winning captivated the city and snagged an unexpected National League East title. The 1989 story line was similar to that of the 1984 club, though the only significant holdovers were '84 MVP Ryne Sandberg and '84 Cy Young winner Rick Sutcliffe. In the meantime, the Cubs had added another

MVP, Andre Dawson, in 1987; stylish homegrown infielders Shawon Dunston and Mark Grace; a wild and crazy bullpen; an intriguing bench; and, before we forget, a change in lighting.

After 75 seasons with only God's own sunshine to illuminate the ballfield—including 40 years as the only major league holdout—Wrigley Field finally saw the light in August 1988. General manager Dallas Green had warned the city that the Cubs would seek new digs if lights continued to be denied Wrigley (a threat backed by Major League Baseball), but Green was not around to see the lights finally turned on. He resigned after the 1987 season due to conflicts with the Tribune Company. Yet the team that Green rebuilt—for a second time—was ready to make a move.

Don Zimmer, fired as third-base coach when Green canned manager Jim Frey in 1986, was named manager in 1988 by Frey, named to replace Green as GM. Frey was no front-office savant. He wound up trading a pitcher who would win 269 games in Jamie Moyer, plus Rafael Palmiero, who would accumulate 3,000 hits and 400 homers (plus a scarlet *S* for lying to Congress about steroids), so the Cubs could acquire a closer to make up for having traded Lee Smith. In Mitch Williams Chicago had its own "Wild Thing"—complete with the same theme song as Charlie Sheen's character in 1989's summer hit *Major League*.

Just as in 1984, the Cubs had a terrible spring training (9–23) and low expectations. This time, however, the Cubs had a homegrown ace. Greg Maddux didn't throw hard and wasn't an overnight success, but by 1989 he had mastered the changeup—and opposing batters. Mike Bielecki won 18 games and Scott Sanderson (the other holdover from 1984) served as swingman. The surprising Cubs spent much of the first half in first place, but it seemed like only a matter of time before the division would be taken over for good by the Mets or Cardinals, who had combined to win five of the last seven division titles (plus one world championship apiece). With a middle-of-the-road $11 million payroll, the Cubs' biggest asset was youth.

Though sprinkled with veterans such as Vance Law, Mitch Webster, Lloyd McClendon, and late-season pickup Luis Salazar, the Cubs also had plenty of up-and-comers age 25 and under: Rookie of the Year Jerome Walton, who had a 30-game hitting streak; ROY runner-up Dwight Smith, who hit .324 in 109 games; plus rookie Joe Girardi, who took over for injured second-year catcher Damon Berryhill. Setup man Les Lancaster had a 1.36 ERA, Mitch Williams led the league

in appearances, the Cubs led the league in saves, and everything Zim tried seemed to work.

Williams opened the season by loading the bases, then fanning the heart of the Phillies order to preserve a one-run lead, establishing a theme for unpredictable yet happy endings. Wild Thing entered in the eighth to squelch a Mets rally, then clubbed a three-run homer in the bottom of the inning for his first major league hit. More happy endings from later in the season: a trick pickoff play between Williams and McLendon ended a one-run win against Montreal; trailing Houston 9–0 in the sixth, the Cubs won, 10–9; tied in extra innings at Wrigley, Rick Wrona, another rookie, laid down a bases-loaded squeeze bunt; after scoring three in the ninth to tie the Giants, the Cubs won when reliever Les Lancaster, an .098 career hitter, singled home the winning run in the 11th; and with their lead down to a half game on September 8, the Cubs won six straight while only once scoring more than four runs. The result? The Cubs took the NL East by six games over the Mets, and seven ahead of the Cardinals.

The 93-win Cubs were a slight favorite in the NL over the 92–70 Giants. And unlike 1984, this NLCS would be best-of-seven, with the Cubs holding home-field advantage. Maddux, who'd

Cubs manager Don Zimmer returns from the locker room to acknowledge the cheers of the crowd after the Cubs defeated the Pittsburgh Pirates 4–1 in the final regular-season home game at Wrigley Field on September 24, 1989.

eschewed going for his 20th win to start Game 1, was hit hard in the first and then harder in the fourth, when Will Clark launched a grand slam for his second home run of the game. The lights—finally in use in October on the North Side—illuminated a few previously concealed faults in an 11–3 trouncing.

Longtime Cub Rick Reuschel finally started a postseason game at Wrigley—as a Giant. Four pitches into the game the Cubs had a single, a double, a triple, and a 2–0 lead. Chicago batted around, scoring six times in the first en route to a 9–5 win. Mark Grace had four hits, giving him six RBIs and seven hits in the first two games.

Les Lancaster, who'd entered Game 3 in midcount in the seventh, allowed a two-run homer when he mistakenly grooved a 2–0 pitch (not the 3–0 pitch he assumed it was). Grace singled to start the eighth, and when Andre Dawson flied to left, Grace hurried back to tag up. Yet Kevin Mitchell's throw was on the money—and there was plenty of room for second-guessing when the next two batters reached base. The Cubs lost 5–4.

Though Maddux was again hit hard, the Cubs knotted Game 4 in the top of the fifth on a triple by Grace and a double by Dawson. Matt Williams bettered that with a two-run homer in the bottom of

A vintage button from 1989's "Wild Bunch"—and what a bunch they were!

the inning off Steve Wilson. Scott Downs was the hero for the Giants, hurling four shutout innings in relief. Steve Bedrosian loaded the bases with two outs in the ninth before fanning Dawson to preserve San Francisco's 6–4 win.

After failing to get out of the first against the Cubs at Wrigley, Rick Reuschel was masterful in Game 5. Mike Bielecki,

LOWER BOX
208 Aisle 1 Row 101 Seat
1990 ALL-STAR GAME®

61ST MIDSUMMER CLASSIC

CHICAGO

1990 CUBS

All·Star Game

AMERICAN LEAGUE
VS
NATIONAL LEAGUE
JULY 10, 1990
7:30 P.M.
WRIGLEY FIELD
ADMIT ONE $50.00
NO REFUND NO EXCHANGE
SUBJECT TO CONDITIONS ON BACK
Aisle 208   Row 1   Seat 101
LOWER BOX

It's been called "a Faustian bargain" and made it possible to sell tickets like this. An agreement between the city, the Cubs, and Major League Baseball to secure lights for Wrigley Field came with a reward—the 1990 All-Star Game, a great *evening* of television for the nation!

however, was winning until a triple by Will Clark and long fly by Kevin Mitchell made it 1–1 in the seventh. Still on the mound in the eighth, Bielecki issued his first three walks of the game—all in a row after two outs—to load the bases for Clark. Mitch Williams came in and Clark sewed up the series MVP— and the NL pennant—with a two-run single.

The series was memorable for the show put on by the two talented young first basemen: Clark batted .650 and Grace .647, with each knocking in eight runs. But the Cubs, a team that relied on late-game heroics all year, wilted in the NLCS as the Giants claimed their first pennant since 1962. If the Cubs had reached their first World Series since 1945, the A's would have been at Wrigley instead of at Candlestick when the massive Bay Area earthquake hit that killed hundreds, caused billions in damage, and postponed the World Series for two weeks. Tragedy outweighs petty concerns, but it would be nearly another decade before Cubs fans could lament more October disappointment.

1990: ALL-STAR CHARM, JUST NOT LUCKY

THE FAUSTIAN BARGAIN between the city, the Cubs, and Major League Baseball to secure lights for Wrigley Field came with a reward for Chicago: the 1990 All-Star Game. Wrigley had seen the Midsummer Classic only twice since *Chicago Tribune* sports editor Arch Ward hatched the idea in 1933. The White Sox got the inaugural game, but the Cubs hosted the event in 1947 and 1962—both American League wins. Those games had been played when it was still a midweek afternoon spectacle. In the late 1960s, however, the All-Star Game went nocturnal, thus excluding Wrigley from hosting duties since those usually went to cities that had built new ballparks. Or at least had lights.

By 1990 Wrigley was equipped for night baseball and even spent $6 million to upgrade the Spartan visitors' clubhouse, plus remodeling the Stadium Club and adding the Sheffield Grill. So on July 10, baseball's big summer stage came to the Friendly Confines. And just like the night the lights first came on in 1988, it rained.

The game was delayed for a total of 85 minutes, including a 68-minute wait in the seventh inning, with Texas Ranger Julio Franco at the plate against Jeff Brantley of the Giants. When the tarp

National League catcher Mike Scioscia of the Dodgers holds up the ball to plate umpire Ed Montague after tagging out Ranger Julio Franco during the seventh inning of the All-Star Game at Wrigley Field on July 11, 1990.

Major League Baseball has a tradition of releasing high-design pins for every All-Star Game. This one commemorates the 1990 game.

came off, Franco faced Rob Dibble of the Reds and promptly doubled home the only two runs of the game to earn game MVP honors. It was one of the few memorable moments from a game with only nine total hits (two by the National League, an All-Star Game record-low). The game even grew more uneventful with time—Reds manager Lou Piniella did not even select the All-Star Game's starting pitcher, Jack Armstrong (1–6 with a 5.96 ERA in the second half), to start against the A's in the 1990 World Series.

Leading up to the first All-Star Game pitch, the flavor was all Chicago. Ryne Sandberg hit the most balls over the ivy in a low-key home-run derby, Ernie Banks threw out the first pitch, and the crowd showered love on Cubs starters Sandberg and Andre Dawson, not to mention reserve Shawon Dunston and Don Zimmer, part of Giants manager Roger Craig's coaching staff. Craig, whose team beat the Cubs in the NLCS the previous fall to gain All-Star manager honors, did not receive a grand reception. Bob Welch, not yet halfway to his 27 wins in 1990, gave Oakland four starters at Wrigley, along with A's manager Tony La Russa filling out the lineup card.

The 2–0 win went to Royals pitcher Bret Saberhagen, one of an economical—by All-Star (and La Russa)

standards—six pitchers used by the AL. Craig employed nine hurlers. Though Bobby Thigpen of the White Sox was on his way to a then-record 57 saves in 1990, La Russa pitched him in the seventh and left the ninth for his own closer, Dennis Eckersley. Pitching at Wrigley for the first time since he was in the Cubs rotation in 1986, Eck got Montreal's Tim Wallach to pop up for the save and give Wrigley Field an 0–3 record for the National League All-Stars.

Armed with lights and fan appeal promises more chances for the NL to get off the schneid at the Friendly Confines.

The high-impact cover of this 1990 All-Star Game program has the official All-Star jewelry pin as its dominant element.

A fan favorite among baseball lovers—and females—during his 15-year career in the majors, MARK GRACE set some records, melted a few hearts, and weathered life's highs and lows—with grace.

Mark Eugene Grace was born in North Carolina in 1964. His childhood was marked by 13 moves in 25 years and a love for baseball that carried over from town to town. He was drafted by the Twins in 1984 but decided to stay in college. The next year, he was drafted by the Cubs and quickly moved from next-to-last line, Single A, Double A, and Triple A. He made his major league debut in May 1988.

Grace was so impressive in his first few weeks that the Cubs traded Leon Durham to the Reds and made Grace the starter at first base. "Amazing" Grace was born. In his rookie year he batted .296 and was named the Sporting News Rookie of the Year. And it only got better.

During the 1989 season, playing with "the Boys of Zimmer," the 6'2" lefty hit .314, with just six errors. While the next eight years were less than stellar for the Cubs, No. 17 consistently batted around .300, resulting in four MVP Awards and three Gold Gloves for Grace.

Grace was beloved by Cubs fans everywhere. But after a couple minor injuries and some clubhouse bickering, management decided not to renew his contract for 2001—without bothering to tell him. After 13 seasons with the Cubs, Grace and the Diamondbacks went to the World Series

This popular baseball card from Topps was "tops" among Cubs fans, who loved the popular first baseman who went on to become the voice of the Cubs on WGN Radio.

MARK GRACE
(1988 – 2000)

1998: THE SEASON OF THRILLS

HOLY COW! HARRY Caray passed away just six weeks before the 1998 season opener. But had he lived just a little longer, the inveterate minstrel of Wrigley Field's famous seventh-inning stretches might have cheered himself to death. On the mound, in the batter's box, and a first-time one-game wild card for the division title made it the Cubs' most exciting season of all time!

From the beginning there were signs that this was no ordinary year of baseball. The Cubs were playing .800 ball after the first 10 games, then a double set of losing streaks plagued the Cubbies in April, but there was lots more to go as May was ushered in. Lots, lots more!

A Rookie Fans 20!

The season was still young on May 6, and so was the Cubs pitcher on that history-making day. Twenty-year-old Kerry Wood turned in one of the most dominant single-game pitching performances

Cubs pitcher Kerry Wood throws a pitch in the second inning against the Milwaukee Brewers on July 10, 1998.

in the history of the game, striking out 20 Houston Astros and allowing just one base hit in a complete-game 2–0 win at Wrigley Field. Wood gave up a single to Ricky Gutierrez in the third inning and hit Craig Biggio with a pitch in the sixth. His 20 strikeouts tied the major league record for a nine-inning game, set twice by Roger Clemens (April 29,1986, and September 18, 1996).

Wood was hurling on one of those gray days with a fine mist in the air, and you couldn't see all that well from the grandstands if you had to look at the distant pitcher's mound. But you *could* see that Kerry had unbelievable stuff that afternoon, including his slider, which looked as if it was breaking two feet. If that's not enough, his curveball was "off the table," as WGN Radio broadcaster Steve Stone put it, "and his fastball was exploding past hitters." The rookie was totally locked in. More surprising, the receiver that day was third-string catcher Sandy Martinez, who was working with Wood for the first time.

It mattered little. The duo made the Astros their most humble of victims, as they went down swinging in fast order:

First: Craig Biggio (swinging), Derek Bell (swinging), Jeff Bagwell (called)

Second: Jack Howell (swinging), Moises Alou (swinging)

CHICAGO **CUBS**

vs.

SAN FRANCISCO **GIANTS**

One-Game Playoff

September 28, 1998 • Wrigley Field

You won't see many of these! The program for the 1998 "Wild Card Night" may be one of the rarest publications in baseball history.

Third: Brad Ausmus (swinging)

Fourth: Bagwell (called), Howell (called)

Fifth: Alou (called), Dave Clark (called), Ricky Gutierrez (called)

Sixth: Shane Reynolds (called)

Seventh: Bagwell (swinging), Howell (swinging), Alou (swinging)

Eighth: Clark (swinging), Gutierrez (swinging), Ausmus (called)

Ninth: Bill Spiers (swinging), Bell (swinging)

Twenty! You can count 'em! Wood opened the game with five straight strikeouts and later had stretches of five and

Cubs slugger Sammy Sosa rips his 63rd home run of the season, a grand slam in the eighth inning, into the left-field grandstand on September 16, 1998.

seven in a row. His stuff was electric, his composure amazing, and his performance simply dazzling. Ron Santo also felt goose bumps early on in the WGN broadcast booth. "I've never felt that way before," he said. "That's the first game I've ever seen that the hitters had no chance."

Sammy Sosa's Home-Run Heroics

The 1998 season echoed the ghosts of the 1961 duel between Yankees teammates Roger Maris and Mickey Mantle in their quest to break Babe Ruth's home-run record. This time it was Sammy Sosa of the Cubs and the St. Louis Cardinals' Mark

In an era when everything has to be bigger and better, along came SAMMY SOSA. He electrified baseball with his enthusiasm for the game—and record-breaking stats. But controversy eventually caught up with the slugger, who in spite of his place atop the record books, may never get elected to the National Baseball Hall of Fame.

Born in 1968 in the Dominican Republic, Sosa played baseball with a milk-carton glove and tree-branch bat. Even then he excelled at the game, getting a minor league contract with the Rangers at age 16—for $3,500.

Despite early struggles, in 1993—his first season with the Cubs—Sosa recorded 33 homers and 93 RBIs. And he was only getting started. The next six years launched a streak of at least 35 home runs and 100 RBIs for No. 21.

His first All-Star appearance was in 1995, and by 1997 he inked a four-season contract worth $42.5 million.

And then came 1998 and the "Home Run Derby." Going head-to-head with the Cardinals' Mark McGwire, Sosa belted 66 homers. McGwire hit 70. It was an exciting time for baseball—and Sosa.

Over the next five years "Slammin' Sammy" became the first player to hit 60 or more home runs in three different seasons and the 18th to hit 500 career homers. But in 2003 injuries and controversy derailed the seven-time All-Star.

Sosa was traded in 2005 and retired in 2007. The once-beloved Cub failed to make the Hall of Fame in 2013—his first year of eligibility. But the legend lives on.

SAMMY SOSA
1993–2005

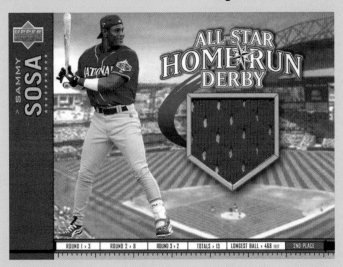

The home-run derby between Sammy Sosa and Mark McGwire permeated baseball. There was even a special-issue baseball card, shown here.

McGwire who were flirting with Maris's record, "61 in '61."

So far in his career Slammin' Sammy's feats in the batter's box included nine consecutive 100-RBI seasons and being the first in Cubs history to post a 30-homer/30-steal season—but those are merely side notes to his prodigious totals during one of the most prolific power runs in baseball history. In 1998 he started a string of six straight 40-plus home-run seasons that included seasons of 66, 63, 50, and 64 round-trippers.

The most indelible moments in Cubs history took place in 1998, though, when Sosa competed with the Cards' Mark McGwire in a yearlong race to set the single-season home-run record. "The great home run chase" captivated baseball fans across the country and added an extra element to a surprising Cubs team that was making an unlikely playoff run. Coming off a season in which he hit only .251, Sosa turned himself into the best all-around hitter in the game that season, lifting his average to .308 and driving in 158 runs.

But the headlines were about the home-run mark. McGwire's 58 homers in 1997 had served notice that he was the man to break Roger Maris's 37-year-old mark of 61 in a season, but after belting 20 home runs in the month of June, Sosa happily made it a two-man race.

The two sluggers traded the home-run lead throughout the summer, but on September 8 in St. Louis, McGwire won the race to 62, breaking Maris's single-season record against the Cubs with a home run off Steve Trachsel. Three days later, well aware that the spotlight had shifted entirely to McGwire, Sosa thrust himself back into the chase with an epic weekend performance in one of the most exciting series ever seen at Wrigley Field.

The Cubs lost the series opener on Friday, falling to the Brewers 13–11, as Sosa hit his 59th home run off Bill Pulsipher. On Saturday the Cubs trailed 10–2 before a rally including Sosa's 60th home run (this one off Valerio de los Santos) led to a 15–12 Cubs win. That wild game ended on Orlando Merced's walk-off homer, but all that was merely a prelude to the excitement of the following day.

With Sosa poised to tie Maris, no one on the North Side cared one bit that McGwire had gotten there first. By game time on Sunday, there was not an inch of available real estate on Waveland Avenue as hundreds of souvenir hunters joined the regular ballhawks hoping to grab a piece of history. Sosa didn't disappoint, tying Maris with his 61st home run in the fifth inning off Bronswell Patrick (there's a trivia-question name for you) as the Cubs built an 8–3 lead. Being the roller-coaster Cubs of '98, Trachsel and Terry Mulholland gave back the lead, and the home team went to the last at-bat down 10–8.

In a season during which he truly was Superman, it strained reality to think that Sosa could come through again in the ninth inning, but he was up to the task. Facing Eric Plunk with a 2–1 count, Sosa launched a no-doubter, bounced out of the batter's box, and watched as his 62nd home run soared over the back fence in left field and landed in between two houses across Waveland. WGN's Chip Caray had the call on Sosa's historic shot: "Swung on, there she goes! Number 62! Move over Big Mac, you've got company!" Left on the sideline five days earlier, Sosa had thrust himself back into the spotlight and a tie for the home-run lead.

With the theme from *The Natural* playing on the public-address system, the ovation continued for six minutes.

The Wild-Card Season Finish

While 1998 was a zinger until the last game of the season, it took an extra day for the Cubs to define the 1998 season. It came down to a single game, an opportunity for redemption, and a memorable evening known forever as "Wild Night" at Wrigley Field. On the season's last day, needing a win to clinch at least a tie for the wild-card spot, the Cubs had stumbled in Houston and lost 4–3 in 11 innings.

As the team limped into the clubhouse, dazed at seeing the year slip away, word from Denver provided the Cubs with a Lazarus-like comeback. Neifi Perez's home run at Coors Field had given the Colorado Rockies an improbable 9–8 win over San Francisco, who ended their season tied with the Cubs.

For the first time since 1980, there would be a game No. 163 on the baseball schedule, and thanks to an earlier coin flip, it would be at Wrigley Field!

That Monday night, September 18, was beyond electric! The Cubs organization left no stone unturned in making it a special night, starting with the decision to tap into positive postseason karma by having Michael Jordan throw out the ceremonial first pitch. Jordan's toss to Sammy Sosa was received with a full-throated roar and ratcheted up the already fevered pitch in the stadium.

The Cubs gave the assignment of saving their season to veteran right-hander Steve Trachsel, while the Giants countered with Mark Gardner. The Cubs got a boost from two-time world-champion third baseman Gary Gaetti, who had just come over from the Cardinals organization on August 19. He provided the first two runs of the night in the fifth inning.

Staked to a 2–0 lead, Trachsel breezed through the sixth inning and saw

It sure looked pretty to fans in 1998!

his cushion double when Matt Mieske's bases-loaded, two-run single in the bottom half of the frame gave the Cubs some breathing room.

Brett Mayne ended Trachsel's no-hitter with a single to right. An ensuing walk chased Trachsel as Matt Karchner came on to face Stan Javier. On the double switch, Orlando Merced was inserted into left field, and proving that the adage "the ball will find you" is especially true in big games, Javier lofted a fly in his direction that hugged the left-field wall. Merced raced over and made a leaping catch that bears an uncanny resemblance to an eerily similar play that Moises Alou wouldn't be able to make five years later. This time, it was the Cubs' night.

Ex-Cub Shawon Dunston singled to load the bases, sending Karchner off and bringing in left-hander Felix Heredia, who faced the daunting task of retiring

Barry Bonds. The brooding Giants star had a history of postseason failure at that point in his career, and he added to the misery by grounding to first to let the Cubs off the hook.

Bill Murray led the crowd in an epic rendition of "Take Me Out to the Ballgame" in the seventh-inning stretch, followed by a Sosa run on a José Mesa wild pitch to give the Cubs a 5–0 lead after eight. Thumbs across Chicago were poised on champagne corks.

Not so fast, though! San Francisco touched Terry Mulholland and Kevin Tapani for two runs to open the ninth, forcing manager Jim Riggleman to go back to his bullpen. Riggleman sent Rod Beck to the mound, needing two outs to send the Cubs to the postseason and the Giants to the golf course.

After a force out of Jeff Kent at second and one more out to go, the Giants'

Joe Carter, the Cubs' No. 1 draft pick in 1981, stepped to the plate. About 10 feet behind the bag, Mark Grace grabbed Carter's pop-up, cradled his head in his hands, and the celebration was on.

An elated Grace jumped gleefully into the stands, and it was just a big lovefest. It didn't take long for the players to go to the clubhouse to grab a few champagne bottles, head back up the runway, and go out on to the field, where a standing-room-only throng was *still* cheering.

Five days later, the Cubs' season would end at Wrigley, swept out of the playoffs by the Atlanta Braves in three anticlimactic games. It didn't matter. For one wild night at Wrigley, the Cubs were champions, but the sentiment "Wail 'til next year" didn't die. Fans' eyes are still on an eventual championship.

Modern Times (2000–2013)

By the 21st century, Chicagoans became used to postseason play at Wrigley Field, with National League Central Division playoffs in 2003, 2007, and 2008. No World Series resulted from the action, but a lot of thrills came with the disappointments!

2003: FROM BOUNTY TO BARTMAN

Though it wasn't usual to see the Cubs logo on postseason jewelry, it was even rarer to see the Marlins' there.

FOLLOWING A 95-LOSS season, manager Don Baylor was out and Dusty Baker was in. Baker had just led the San Francisco Giants to the NL pennant and brought with him an aura of confidence that had previously been absent on the North Side.

The Cubs rode their handful of aces to the brink of an NL Central championship. The combination of Kerry Wood, Mark Prior, Carlos Zambrano, and Matt Clement put the Cubs in a position to win in nearly every one of their outings. All four stayed healthy, pitched more than 200 innings, and they won. Shawn Estes was the only starter to post less than 13 *W*s.

After going 19–8 in September, their final three-game home stand against the lowly Pittsburgh Pirates was all that stood between them and an NL Central title.

After the first game was rained out, manager Dusty Baker handed the ball to Prior for the rescheduled game the next day (to be played back-to-back with the second game against the Pirates). The 23-year-old "can't-miss" prospect was in the middle of the finest season of his career, posting a team-high 18 wins and finishing third in the NL Cy Young voting. From his first pitch of the afternoon, Prior knew

A unique look at the infamous Bartman debacle, from behind the doomed fan.

that the feeling in the Friendly Confines was special. "It was just one of those days," Prior said. "I threw the ball in the dirt and received a standing ovation." Prior gave up two runs on eight hits, allowing the Cubs to cruise to a 4–2 victory and a chance to clinch the division by winning the second game of the day.

In the second game Chicago found themselves with a 7–2 lead in the top of the ninth, the 40,121 Cubby blue–clad fans were bubbling with excitement and antici-pation. Then, with one out and the Pirates' Jason Bay on first, the crowd was ready to reach a crescendo.

Pirates third baseman Jose Hernandez hit a weak ground ball to Cubs shortstop Alex Gonzalez. Gonzalez calmly flipped the ball to Grudzielanek at second. Grudzielanek whipped the ball over to first baseman Eric Karros, completing the game-ending double play and punching Chicago's ticket to play October baseball once again.

A dog pile formed at the pitch-er's mound as Wrigley Field erupted with an array of yells, whistles, and screams. Celebratory champagne was given out as Sammy Sosa sprinted out to right field to douse the Bleacher Bums in bubbly. Like Ernie Banks said nearly 50 years prior, September 27, 2003, truly proved to be a "good day to play two."

The Playoffs

After a back-and-forth NLDS against the Braves gave the Cubs their first postseason series victory since 1908, Chicago was primed to face the Florida Marlins in the NLCS.

The Cubs dropped Game 1 but won the next three. After a dominating performance by Florida's Josh Beckett in Game 5, the Cubs were headed back to Chicago with a 3–2 series lead and Prior and Wood poised to start. Two chances to get one win and erase 58 years of being left out of the World Series party.

In the eighth inning of Game 6, Prior was in rare form, the defense was stout, and the Cubs had a three-run lead with five outs to go. What happened next was, unfortunately, a series of events that would come to define the 2003 Chicago Cubs season.

The Bartman Ball

There were 37,415 fans crammed into Wrigley Field that October night, but Moises Alou was pointing at only one. That fan was Steve Bartman. It was Bartman's outstretched hands that had made their way between Luis Castillo's fly ball and Alou's glove. Every fan around him had reached for the ball, attempting to take home a piece of what they thought would be a historic event, but it was the man sitting in Section 4,

Talented? Very much so. But the star pitcher's reputation as a hothead has also landed CARLOS ZAMBRANO on a list of "Five MLB Free Agents You Don't Want Near Your Clubhouse."

Cubs fans loved Zambrano—on a good day. And there were many. He worked as both a starter and a closer and had success in both roles. In 2008 the right-handed pitcher threw a no-hitter against the Astros. And if his pitching accomplishments weren't enough, the switch-hitter's career batting average was a respectable .231, and he holds the record for the most career home runs by a Cubs pitcher at 23.

The 6'4" Venezuelan debuted with the Cubs in 2001. In his first full season as a starter in 2003, he registered 168 strikeouts and a 3.11 ERA. He became the only National League pitcher with 13 wins in every year from 2003 to 2008. Not too shabby.

But when his performance wasn't up to par, Zambrano had a hard time accepting any blame. He notoriously blamed teammates for the team's troubles and wasn't afraid to get physical about it. In 2007 he got in a fight with catcher Michael Barrett that started in the dugout and continued in the locker room.

An altercation with an umpire in 2009 got him ejected—and later suspended. And a fight with first baseman Derrek Lee in 2010 earned him six weeks in anger management. By 2011 his temper was interfering with his pitching more and more, and the Big Z was finally traded to the Miami Marlins in 2012.

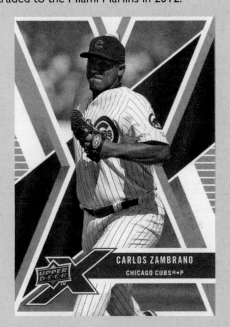

This Upper Deck card for Carlos Zambrano has a distinctive "21st-century look," which distinguishes its design from early baseball cards..

CARLOS ZAMBRANO (2001–2012)

Row 8, Seat 113 who would take the blame. As Alou screamed at left-field umpire Mike Everitt to call fan inference, gesturing toward the man in the green turtleneck, glasses, and headphones, the tension inside Wrigley started to rise. With no Jumbotron to show a replay, those inside the ballpark who didn't have a clear view of the play weren't quite sure what happened. Those watching faithfully

The 2003 NLCS program features all the Cubs stars: Sosa, Prior, Wood, and Alou.

at home had the unfortunate luxury of watching the agonizing play over and over again, as FOX's play-by-play announcer Thom Brennaman said what every Cubs fan was thinking: "It's safe to say that every Cubs fan has to be wondering right now, *Is the Curse of the Billy Goat alive and well?*"

As word around the ballpark spread that it was Bartman who had interfered with Alou's catch, the Friendly Confines turned chaotic. Fans screamed expletives, tossed debris, and made threats on Bartman's life. Bartman was ushered out of the ballpark, but not before a fan poured an entire beer on the man who was simply trying to do what all baseball fans are conditioned to do— catch a foul ball.

Bartman's life was completely altered due to the incident; he became the biggest Chicago villain since Al Capone. The Little League baseball coach from Northbrook, IL, has gone down in Chicago baseball infamy, adding to the string of cursed *B*s that have plagued the Cubs through the years. There was the billy goat, the black cat, and now Bartman.

However, after the mayhem subsided, the count was still 3–2, center fielder Juan Pierre was still on second base, and the five outs needed to win the pennant remained.

What happened after the Bartman Ball was much worse than a case of uncalled fan interference.

After Louis Castillo walked, Marlins catcher Ivan Rodriguez hit a line drive into left field. Pierre scored, and Florida had life.

Then Miguel Cabrera hit a high bouncing ground ball to Cubs shortstop Alex Gonzalez. With Gonzalez's sure-handedness and Cabrera's lack of speed, it seemed to be a textbook double play. Gonzalez, who led all National League shortstops in fielding percentage, tried to backhand the ball, fumbled it, and watched as the ball fell to the ground. All runners were safe and the rally continued.

A two-run double, a sacrifice fly, a three-run double, and an RBI single later, the score was 8–3. The Cubs still had two half-innings to make up the deficit, but it didn't matter. Their will was broken. The eighth inning of Game 6 proved to be an inning from which the Cubs would never recover.

In Game 7 and with Wood on the mound, Chicago jumped out to a 5–3 lead in the fourth inning. However, the Marlins would not be denied, responding in the sixth and seventh to go ahead 9–5. A Troy O'Leary home run in the seventh was useless. The Cubs' fate was sealed. As much as it looked like 2003 would be the year, it simply wasn't. The Marlins celebrated as the Cubs sulked into the dugout, preparing for a World Series–less off-season that felt all too familiar.

2005: GREG MADDUX'S 3,000TH STRIKEOUT

BASEBALL PLAYERS AND fans talk about respect more than Aretha Franklin, but occasionally they get it right. Greg Maddux, the four-time Cy Young Award winner and Cubs prodigal son, received that respect of the highest level on a rainy night in July 2005, when more than 30,000 Cubs fans braved the elements and a long rain delay in order to see him get his 3,000th strikeout.

They had waited a long time to honor one of their favorites. At age 22, Maddux was the Cubs' youngest All-Star in 1988, led the team to a division title in 1989, and was clearly a star on the rise, with an understanding of the game that was not lost on his teammates. "He was a great teacher," noted catcher Joe Girardi. "I was a young player and he was a young player—he's actually younger than I am—but he had been up. He was a great teacher and was always willing to offer advice, talk about how to get hitters out. When I think of Greg Maddux, I think of a guy who studied the game as hard as any player I've ever been around, never missed anything, was always on the bench, paid attention to detail, and that's what made him so great."

When it came time for a long-term contract after his Cy Young

This unassuming-looking ticket—probably generated by machine, rather than printed in color like the usual Cubs tickets—defies its importance as Wrigley Field memorabilia. The ticket is for the historic 2005 game in which Greg Maddux achieved his 3,000th strikeout.

"MADDUX" by Bill Lopa

/3000

NATIONAL
Sports Collectors Convention

Artist Bill Lopa—obviously influenced by renowned painter LeRoy Neiman—captures the intensity of Greg Maddux on the mound!

guidance for the team's young guns Carlos Zambrano, Kerry Wood, and Mark Prior.

Jim Hendry relayed a typical Maddux story during spring training in 2005. "Greg was standing on the side with some of our young pitchers. Whoever was on the mound was really bringing it and got some *ooohs* and *ahhhs* after a few good fastballs. Greg said to them, 'If you're standing on the side of the road and a truck races by, can you tell me if it's going 85 or 95 miles per hour? It's not about speed.'"

The previous year, Maddux had become the 22nd pitcher to win 300 games, but that victory happened in San Francisco, not at Wrigley Field. So when Maddux went into his start on July 26, 2005, two strikeouts shy of the 3,000 mark, Cubs fans readied themselves to share the moment with their hero. "The interesting thing about that night was we had a rain delay," said play-by-play announcer Len Kasper. "It would have been an easy night for the regular fans who come out or the season-ticket holders to not hang around for the entire night, but they did."

Like so many other facets of Cubs fandom, it was no piece of cake. The start of the game was delayed two hours and 43 minutes by rain, but in tribute to Maddux, a full house stayed through the downpour to make sure they were on hand for his milestone. (Maybe the greatest tribute is

Award–winning 1992 season, the Cubs allowed their ace to be lured away by the Atlanta Braves. Twelve years, three more Cy Youngs, one World Series ring, and 194 victories later, Maddux re-signed with the Cubs to bolster what promised to be a sturdy rotation as well as to provide

Cubs starting pitcher Greg Maddux throws during the first inning against the San Francisco Giants on Tuesday, July 26, 2005, at Wrigley Field. Maddux got one strikeout during the inning for the 2,999th of his career.

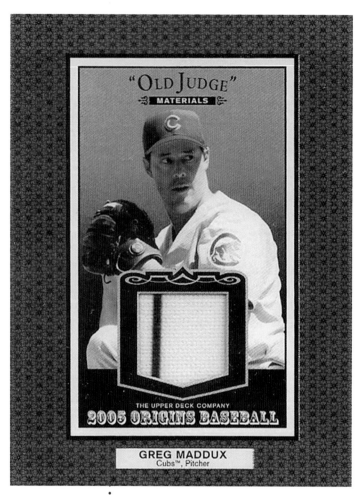

GREG MADDUX
Cubs™, Pitcher

The Upper Deck company designed this 2005 Greg Maddux card to look like their old-time cards from the 1880s, which used sepia-tone photographic albumen prints.

erupted. After walking straight to the dug-out, Maddux smiled sheepishly and finally allowed himself to be pushed out for a curtain call as the standing ovation continued.

From his perch in the booth, Bob Brenly soaked in the moment. "That's something that you may never see again," said Brenly, who contributed two punchouts to the Maddux total during his playing career. "Certainly it's possible that we'll never see it again at Wrigley Field. For everything that Greg Maddux did for this team, for everything that Greg Maddux did for the game of baseball, those fans wanted to be sure that when that moment came, they were here. There could have been lightning striking the towers, there could have been snow falling, they were going to stay until he got that strikeout and show their appreciation, and that's the kind of fans they are."

Manning first base that night, Derrek Lee marveled at his teammate's achievement. "Greg Maddux is a guy who commands respect wherever he goes, and I think the fans respect him tremendously," said Lee. "They wanted to be here to see him get that 3,000th strikeout, and they gave him a standing ovation. It was a great moment." In the dugout, Kerry Wood understood the cheers were especially heartfelt. "It's just the respect for him," Wood said. "The fans wanted to

that beer sales had stopped well before the first pitch, but the crowd stayed anyway.) In typical Maddux fashion, he wasted no time, putting away Jason Ellison to lead off the game. Two innings later, with two outs, Maddux painted the corner on Omar Vizquel for number 3,000, and the crowd

show their respect for him, and they sat through the rain. The umpires didn't want to call that game. They said, 'We're gonna get it in.' It was a special night, it really was."

There was a fitting Cubs symmetry in Maddux's accomplishment of becoming the second man in major league history to strike out 3,000 batters while yielding fewer than 1,000 walks. The first man, Fergie Jenkins, also wore No. 31 during his years with the Cubs. "I've got to quit before I hit 1,000 walks," joked Maddux. "It was a very nice moment," he admitted. "You know, I've never really considered myself a strikeout pitcher. I've always thought strikeouts were overrated, to be honest with you. You've got to get 27 outs. You don't have to get 12 strikeouts and give up five runs to do it, you know what I mean? Strikeouts to me have always been overrated. To pitch long enough to get that many strikeouts is special, and I'm just kind of glad I've hung around for as long as I have."

Numbers don't drive Greg Maddux. Wins and championships do. But he did allow himself a smile when asked about that night and the response from the Cubs fans. "They are special people. It's just an honor and a privilege to play here. It always has been."

As pretty as it was to look at, Cub fans still cried, "Next year!"

2007 SEASON: FROM EMBERS TO FLAMES

FOLLOWING A SEASON in which they finished last in the National League, the Cubs were in dire need of restructuring. After guiding Chicago to a paltry 66 wins, manager Dusty Baker was given the boot. Cubs general manager Jim Hendry needed a big-name replacement for Baker if Chicago had any chance of rebuilding their team and returning to the postseason. The search was short, only three weeks, and finished sweet as Lou "Sweet Lou" Piniella was signed on to right the Cubs' sinking ship. Piniella brought with him a winning legacy: he had led the Reds

COMMEMORATIVE NLDS SCORECARD
WRIGLEY FIELD • OCTOBER 4-7, 2007

CHICAGO VS ARIZONA

NLDS

With the Cubs doing their spring training in Arizona, at least they could be in familiar territory for the 2007 NLDS.

to the World Series in 1990 and was the AL Manager of the Year twice while in Seattle.

The Cubs added small pieces by trading for reliever Neal Cotts and signing utility man Mark DeRosa, but they were still looking to sign a marquee free agent to show the baseball world that they were through being the bottom feeders of the National League. Chicago caught their big fish in outfielder Alfonso Soriano. The sweet-swinging righty was coming off the best season of his career, hitting 46 home runs and stealing 41 bases, to become the fourth member of the elusive 40-40 club. Soriano was a special player, and the Cubs treated him like one, offering him an eight-year, $136 million contract—the most Chicago had ever offered a player in the franchise's history.

Although expectations for the team were low, a new manager and a new superstar had Cubs fans believing that they could at least be competitive in 2007. However, the flashy off-season acquisitions failed to pay off to start the season. Soriano seemed to be a bust, hitting only .270 with zero home runs, and Piniella was failing to find a winning combination amongst the scraps left from the abysmal 2006 season, as Chicago stumbled out to a 22–29 record. The first two months of the season saw the Cubs struggle to beat up on any team, and as June began, Chicago turned their

Lou Piniella glowers from under the brim of his cap during a game against the Cardinals on September 18, 2009.

Alfonso Soriano connects with the ball for a two-run double against the Los Angeles Dodgers during the seventh inning of a game on August 5, 2012.

fighting efforts away from the National League and toward themselves.

The June 1 game against the Atlanta Braves was looking like just another game. Chicago found themselves down early, dropped two pop flies, and starting pitcher Carlos Zambrano ended his outing having given up seven runs on 13 hits, most of which came in a fifth inning that saw five Braves cross home plate. In the fifth, after the third out was finally made, Zambrano went back to the dugout, arms flailing and expletives streaming from his mouth. Big Z looked like a bull that had just seen red, and unfortunately his battery mate became the matador. Zambrano charged at catcher Michael Barrett, turning the Cubs dugout into a back-alley street fight. A stiff right hook from Zambrano cut Barrett's lip, and the two exchanged words and punches before being separated by their teammates. To add insult to Barrett's injury, the 8–5 loss was Chicago's fifth straight.

The day after the clubhouse melee, Piniella got into a tussle of his own. After outfielder Angel Pagan was caught stealing in the eighth inning, the Cubs manager threw a temper tantrum that would put any five-year-old to shame. Piniella kicked dirt, threw his hat, and huffed and puffed after third-base umpire Mark Wegner ejected him from the game. Piniella walked off the field as the Wrigley Field crowd roared with applause. Up to that point, it was one of the few moments that elicited cheers from the Wrigley Field crowd all season.

The Cubs were in bad shape. They had players who were more concerned with beating each other than the other team, a manager who couldn't keep his cool, and a season that already looked to be beyond saving. Chicago seemed destined to spend October at home for the fourth straight year.

Then, with no warning or explanation, Chicago began to catch fire. The team that earlier in the season couldn't keep their hands off one another or catch a fly ball suddenly couldn't lose. Piniella, who had weathered the media's disdain all year for putting such a young unproven team on the field, now looked like the smartest manager in the league. Three rookies—shortstop Ryan Theriot, second baseman Mike Fontenot, and catcher Geovany Soto—finally shed their growing pains and became three of Chicago's most important players. Soriano bounced back from his disappointing start and finally morphed into the dangerous offensive threat the Cubs hoped he could be. The three young bucks, the superstar, and the main holdovers from the 2006 team, Derrek Lee and Aramis Ramirez, were finally coming together. Maybe Piniella knew what he was doing when he got ejected by Wegner. Maybe he didn't. Either way, the ejection lit a fire underneath his group of former underachievers. Chicago went 63–46 after June 3, storming their way to the NL Central title and their first postseason appearance since 2003.

The Cubs were hot and looked to be the favorites in the NLDS against the Arizona Diamondbacks. Zambrano, who had bounced back from his stint as an amateur clubhouse boxer to lead Chicago with 18 wins, had the task of stifling an already weak Arizona offense, as the Diamondbacks were last in the NL in batting average.

While Zambrano was good, striking out eight and giving up only one run through six innings, Arizona's Brandon Webb was better. The NL Cy Young runner-up baffled Chicago's hitters, striking out nine in seven innings to give Arizona their first win of the series, 3–1.

In Game 2, the Cubs' adolescent behavior once again reared its ugly head. After hanging a pitch that Chris Young promptly launched to left field, Chicago pitcher Ted Lilly spun around and ferociously spiked his glove to the Chase Field turf. This wasn't a good sign. The Cubs were light years away from the type of behavior that had plagued them in the first part of the season. However, as the temper tantrums returned, so did the disappointing results. Arizona took Game 2, and the Cubs faced the daunting task of overcoming a 0–2 deficit in a postseason series for the sixth time in franchise history. The Cubs' record in those previous series was 0–5.

Any momentum that the Cubs might have had by returning to Wrigley Field was quickly sucked out of the Friendly Confines as Young led off the game with a solo home run off Cubs pitcher Rich Hill. Arizona added another run in the first off of a Justin Upton single and never looked back, closing the book on the Cubs season with a 5–1 victory.

Although Chicago's season ended in disappointment, the silver linings were certainly there. This was a team that was expected to fail but became the biggest surprise in the National League. They had bright young players to build around, a powerful offense, and a manager that was just the right amount of crazy. Cubs fans for the last 100 years told themselves, "Wait 'til next year." The only difference now was that they had a reason to wait.

Born in a country where baseball is king, ALFONSO SORIANO is certainly a prince among men. But it wasn't always that way for the outfielder from the Dominican Republic.

Like his uncle and two brothers before him, Soriano knew baseball was his ticket to the good life. Born in 1976, he was actually slow and awkward in his younger years, and when Hilario, Julio, and Frederico never made it beyond the minor leagues, there was little hope that Alfonso would surpass them. So on his 16th birthday he signed with a Japanese farm club.

He hated the "life" but loved the baseball and quickly developed his on-field skills. His star on the rise, he retired from Japanese ball and came to the US to become a free agent. As he improved—tremendously—he switched teams and positions many times before the Cubs signed him to an eight-year $136 million deal starting in 2007. In his first year as a Cub he finished with a .299 batting average, leading the team in home runs, triples, and runs scored.

After a great start, Soriano had three poor seasons riddled with errors and hitting woes. But in 2012 he returned to form—hitting 32 home runs and driving in 108 runs while batting .262.

Baseball aficionados refer to Soriano's "it" factor as an "intangible." And that intangible has taken this 6'1" right-hander to great heights. He says he wants to remain with the Cubs to the end, and while trade talks swirl, his contract gives him the last word. And he just wants to have fun.

This Soriano baseball card has the distinctive soft colors and old-time look that has reemerged on many cards issued during the 21st century.

ALFONSO SORIANO
(2007–2013)

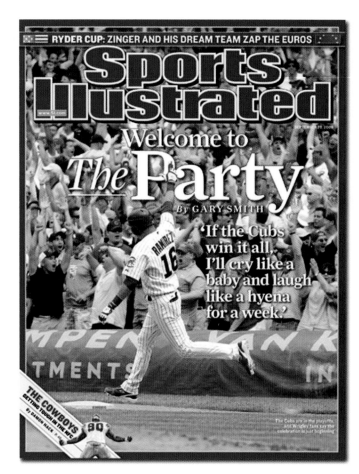

By midseason 2008 everyone was optimistic that this would be the year, even *Sports Illustrated*.

2008 SEASON: A TRAGIC CENTENNIAL

THE 2008 SEASON marked an anniversary for the Chicago Cubs organization, but no one celebrated.

It had been an even century since the Cubs had last won a World Series. The symmetry was both encouraging and alarming. If there was a year to end the drought, this was surely it. On the other hand, Chicago's recurring World Series absence served as an embarrassing reminder that the Cubs were on the top of the pyramid of baseball futility.

Ironically, as the Curse of the Billy Goat teetered on triple digits, the Cubs had one of their best years in franchise history. Chicago posted 97 wins, good enough for the best record in the National League, the most for a Cubs team since they last won the pennant, in 1945. The Cubs' second consecutive trip to the postseason also marked the first time they had achieved such a feat since their last championship season, in 1908.

Before the season began, Chicago looked across the Pacific to increase their offensive firepower, winning the bid for former Chunichi Dragons outfielder Kosuke Fukudome. Although Fukudome was coming off elbow surgery and the worst season in his baseball career, he was still expected to bring even more punch to an already stout Chicago offense. Fukudome joined outfielder Alfonso Soriano, first baseman Derrek Lee, and third baseman Aramis Ramirez on a Cubs offense that was poised to be among the league's best.

The Cubs started 2008 hot, racking up two different five-game winning streaks in the season's first month. Their second winning streak was highlighted by a 7–6 win over the Colorado Rockies in 10 innings on April 23. The win put Chicago in rare company with the San Francisco Giants, making them the only franchise to reach 10,000 wins other than the club that used to call the Polo Grounds home.

That hot streak continued into the All-Star break. Chicago snatched up first place on May 12 and never conceded the top line for the rest of the year. Baseball fans rewarded Chicago's early season success as a record-tying eight Cubs were elected to the All-Star team. Fukodome, Soriano, and Geovany Soto were all named as starters, Aramis Ramirez was subbed in at third base, and Carlos Zambrano, Ryan Dempster, and Carlos Marmol all came on in relief. Kerry Wood was the lone Cubs All-Star not to play in the game, due to a blister on his finger.

While Chicago's offense helped the Cubs obtain National League dominance in the first half of the season, it was their pitching in the second half that allowed them to maintain it. Ryan Dempster continued to be phenomenal, closing out the season with 17 wins and 187 strikeouts and looked to be the ace that the Cubs could rely on in October. A trade for Oakland's Rich Harden in July gave Chicago the perfect complement to Dempster's brilliance. After settling into his new home on the North Side, the former Athletic posted a 1.77 ERA and 89 strikeouts in 71 innings. Dempster was proving reliable, Harden became explosive, but it was Zambrano who started to make 2008 feel magical.

On September 14 the righty from Venezuela tossed the first Cubs no-hitter since 1972. As if breaking a 36-year-old record wasn't enough, the no-no against the Houston Astros was the first one to be thrown at a neutral site: the game was played at Milwaukee's Miller Park in the aftermath of Hurricane Ike.

Making history and breaking records? These were the types of changes of fortune that Cubs fans were happy to see.

Chicago finally clinched the Central division on September 20 with a 5–4 win over the St. Louis Cardinals, finishing the season seven and a half games ahead of the second-place Milwaukee Brewers. The Cubs also had a winning

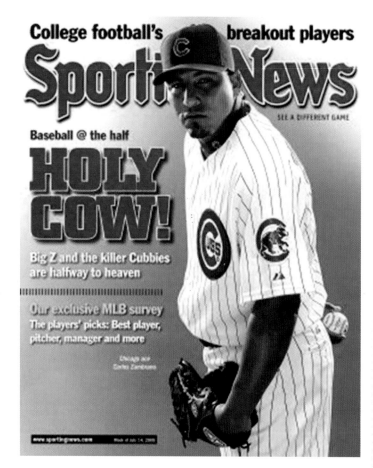

Around the All-Star break, *The Sporting News* implied that 2008 *might* indeed be the year!

record against every other National League team and looked to be the overwhelming favorite going into the playoffs.

Greeting the Cubs in their second consecutive trip to the postseason were the Los Angeles Dodgers. With emotions at Wrigley running high and Dempster on the hill, Chicago was poised to win their first playoff game since 2003. Mark DeRosa started off the party by smashing a ball into the right-field bleachers in the second inning to put the Cubs ahead 2–0.

Unfortunately for Chicago, those were the only runs they would score all game.

A James Loney grand slam in the fifth knocked Dempster out of the game, and the Dodgers cruised to a 7–2 victory. Dusk greeted the Friendly Confines as Cubs fans wandered out into the frigid Wrigleyville evening, hoping that Game 2 would produce a different outcome.

Unfortunately for Chicago, the second game of the NLDS proved to be as dreadful as the first. Although Chicago seemed to have the upper hand over the Dodgers in almost every facet of the game, there was one thing they simply could not account for: the unstoppable postseason phenomenon known as "Manny Being Manny."

Los Angeles left fielder Manny Ramirez had his fair share of questionable

Zambrano truly made 2008 magical.

moments during his baseball career; however, his dominance in the postseason was an absolute truth. In Game 2, Ramirez hit his second home run of the 2008 postseason, his 26th of his playoff career, setting an all-time record. Ramirez added a single in the eighth inning as Chicago's offense, which had been so dominant all season, refused to get on track, only mustering three runs against Dodgers starter Chad Billingsley. The Dodgers closed out Game 2 10–3, with thoughts of going back and completing the sweep at Chavez Ravine on their mind.

As the series moved back to Los Angeles, the Dodgers were attempting to finish off the Cubs. And close out they did. Loney, the hero for the Dodgers in Game 1, hit a two-run double in the first inning, and Russell Martin added a double of his own in the fifth to put Los Angeles ahead 3–0. A Daryle Ward RBI single in the eighth was Chicago's last attempt at a comeback, but it wasn't be enough.

Alas, 2008 would not end up being the year that the curse was cured. Chicago was sent home from Los Angeles, relegated to watching another team lift the World Series trophy. It was back to the drawing board for the Cubs, trying to find a way to make sure that 100 didn't become 101.

THE CRY THAT NEVER DIES: "WAIT 'TIL NEXT YEAR!"

*W*HILE THE CHICAGO Cubs were trying unsuccessfully to claim a third straight National League Central Division title in 2009, a 35-year-old Theo Epstein was guiding the fate of the Boston Red Sox as general manager, just two summers removed from that franchise's second World Series championship in four seasons. The Cubs and Red Sox—long known as baseball's "lovable losers"—were about to have more in common than their legacy of frustration.

Epstein's Red Sox made the playoffs as a wild card in '09, while the Cubs spent 17 days atop the standings that year but fell short in their bid to join Boston in the postseason. Manager Lou Piniella's club fielded one of the best infields in baseball—sluggers Aramis Ramirez and Derrek Lee at the corners with former LSU teammates Mike Fontenot and Ryan Theriot patrolling the middle—but the Cardinals were eight wins better in the '09 standings.

It marked the last time the Cubs posted a winning record (83–78), and the resulting tumble set in motion a series of events that brought Epstein, once the youngest GM in the history of Major League Baseball at age 28, from Boston to

Chicago. It began with the announcement in October 2009 that the Tribune Company would sell the Cubs to Tom Ricketts and family. Tom, the son of Ameritrade founder J. Joseph Ricketts and educated at the University of Chicago, got into baseball to bring a winner to the Windy City. And he was keenly aware of how the Red Sox turned their fate around.

Cubs fans would just as soon forget the 2010 and 2011 seasons. During the former, Piniella decided he had endured enough. The longtime major league outfielder and three-time Manager of the Year (twice in the AL and once in the NL) had arrived in 2007 with high hopes of being the man who would lead the Cubs to their first World Series title since 1908. He resigned with his club at 51–74. His replacement, Mike Quade, won 24 of 37 games down the stretch, but it was a mirage—a short-term run of success made against several teams that had packed it in for the season. Quade's 71–91 record in 2011 was a better indication of where the Cubs stood, particularly after they dumped several top players during the '09 plunge.

The Cubs needed a change in direction. Up in Boston, Epstein was contemplating his next challenge. Could the wunderkind who helped the Red Sox end their 86-year championship drought in 2004 rescue another downtrodden franchise more than a century removed from its last World Series crown? When he accepted his post as Cubs president of baseball operations in October 2011, that's precisely the challenge for which he signed up.

Cubs fans everywhere lauded the hiring of Epstein. If he could do it in Boston, they surmised, surely he could win in Chicago. However, even the most ambitious among the North Side faithful recognized that there would be no easy fix. The talent on the big-league club did not stack up with that of the National League contenders, and there was no stable of farm-system horses waiting to be turned loose.

New manager Dale Sveum had his hands full. The 2012 Cubs lost 101 times, their first 100-loss season since 1966. It was not exactly a summer of hope, unless you knew whom to ask.

"I think the progress is tremendous," Ricketts said, a nod to the work Epstein and his staff began doing in that first year. "People can't see all the decisions that are made behind the scenes. I see these guys making hundreds of smart decisions during the course of the year. Some of them are public decisions, and a lot of them are smaller decisions made behind the scenes. I just have complete, total confidence that they are moving us in the right direction."

Theo Epstein looks up into the
Wrigley Field stands before the
start of Opening Day 2012.

The former owner of the Cubs, the Tribune Company, emblazoned on the front page of their paper that, by 2014—the centennial year of Wrigley Field—there might be something new to see at the ballpark.

"I'll tell about one of my best days of the year last year," Epstein recalled during 2013 spring training. "I was walking on the field of our instructional league. We had our new farm director, our new field coordinator, our coaches, our young players...the energy they were putting out was off the charts. We had a talented group of young players who were clearly proud to be Cubs, who cared for each other, who were playing hard after a long season, pulling for each other, competing with each other."

It was the kind of pride Epstein wants to see from every player, coach, manager, and member of the franchise. It's a pride the Cubs faithful display day after day with their patronage. Despite suffering through more losses than all but one team (Houston) in the majors in 2012, the Cubs drew almost 2.9 million fans to Wrigley Field—a phenomenon Epstein chalks up, in part, to the team's reputation as "lovable losers." It's a reputation he longs to eradicate.

"I think that's also an opportunity," Epstein said in 2013. "I tell the players, 'Right now, we're called lovable losers. What do you want to stand for?'"

I guarantee you if you ask the guys, they don't want to be known as lovable losers three or four years from now."

The 2013 season is the Cubs' last before Wrigley Field celebrates its 100th birthday. By the time the Friendly Confines turn a century old, the team's new leaders expect the longstanding refrain of Cubs fans—"Wait 'til next year!"—to be a legitimate warning to National League contenders that the lovable losers are about to win big.

SOURCES:

Part I:

http://www.examiner.com/article/the-history-of-wrigleyville.
http://www.chicagotraveler.com/neighborhoods/wrigleyville-feature.htm.
research.sabr.org/journals/building-of-wrigley-field.
http://www.nps.gov/nhl/DOE_dedesignations/wrigley.htm.
http://sports.espn.go.com/espnmag/story?id=3518172.
http://www.businessweek.com/stories/2004-10-26/bill-veeck-a-baseball-mastermind.
http://www.ballparksofbaseball.com/nl/WrigleyField.htm.
http://chicago.cubs.mlb.com/chc/ballpark/information/index.jsp?content=history.
http://www.baseball-almanac.com/stadium/wrigley_field.shtml.
http://chicago.cubs.mlb.com/chc/history/timeline04.jsp.
http://www.thecalledshot.com/thecalledshot.com/Home.html.
http://mlb.mlb.com/content/printer_friendly/chc/y2007/m07/d20/c2099223.jsp.
http://www.ebbets.com/product/ChicagoWhales1915HomeJersey/BaseballJerseys.

PART II:
1918: First Place Just Wasn't Good Enough:
Baseball Almanac: http://www.baseball-almanac.com/ws/yr1918ws.shtml.
New York Times. "Cubs Check Foe in Second Game of Title Series: Batting and
    Pitching of Tyler Give Chicago Victory Over Red Sox by 3–1." Special Section,
    September 7, 1918.
Snyder, John. *Cubs Journal*. Cincinnati: Emmis Books, 2005 (pgs. 199–201).

Pete Alexander Sidebar:
 http://www.bleedcubbieblue.com/2007/1/26/93224/4732.
http://www.baseball-reference.com/players/a/alexape01.shtml.

Gabby Hartnett Sidebar:
http://baseballhall.org/hof/hartnett-gabby.
http://sabr.org/bioproj/person/ab6d173e.
http://www.baseball-almanac.com/players/player.php?p=hartnga01.

1922: Cubs Defeat Phillies in 49-Run Slugfest:

Christian Science Monitor. http://www.csmonitor.com/USA/Sports/2012/0405/MLB-Opening-Day-Looking-back-at-100-years-of-baseball-history/1922.

Jason Stark Blog, ESPN.com: https://www.google.com/search?q=Single-game+stunners+Aug+.+25+%2C+1922&ie=utf-8&oe=utf-8&aq=t&rls=org.mozilla:en-US:official&client=firefox-a.

New York Times. "Cubs and Phillies Smash 2 Records: Chicago Team Wins Weird Game in Which 51 Hits Are Made, 26–23," August 26, 1922.

Yahoo Sports. "Highest Scoring Games in Major League Baseball History": http://sports.yahoo.com/mlb/news?slug=ycn-8700635.

1929: Domination Turns to Doom:

Chastain, Bill. *Hack's 191: Hack Wilson and His Incredible 1930 Season*. Guilford, CT: Globe Pequot Press, 2012 (pgs. 13–24).

Levy, Alan H. *Joe McCarthy: Architect of the Yankee Dynasty*. Jefferson, NC: McFarland & Co., 2005 (pgs. 125–40).

New York Times. "Cubs Clinch Flag, Tough Beaten, 7–3," September 19, 1929.

Snyder, John. *Cubs Journal*. Cincinnati: Emmis Books, 2005 (pgs. 253–53).

Part III:
1932: Babe's Called Shot:

Excerpted with permission from Krantz, Les. *Yankee Classics: World Series Magic from the Bronx Bombers—1921 to Today*. Minnesota: MVP Books, 2010.

Hack Wilson Sidebar:

http://www.bleedcubbieblue.com/2007/1/28/5501/22175.
http://chicago.cubs.mlb.com/chc/history/chc_feature_wilson.jsp.
http://baseballhall.org/hof/wilson-hack.
http://www.thedeadballera.com/BeerDrinkersHackWilson.html.

1935: Sizzling Streak Produces 100 Wins, World Seroes Berth:

http://www.youtube.com/watch?v=cCFUEqV_ZZ4 (Series video highlights).

http://www.rarenewspapers.com/view/588250.

http://blog.detroitathletic.com/2011/10/25/the-hit-that-won-the-tigers-first-world-series-title/.

http://mlb.mlb.com/mlb/history/postseason/mlb_ws_recaps.jsp?feature=1935.

http://www.time.com/time/magazine/article/0,9171,755165,00.html.

http://www.baseball-reference.com/postseason/1935_WS.shtml.

http://muse.jhu.edu/journals/nin/summary/v013/13.2goss.html.

http://articles.chicagotribune.com/1986-04-13/features/8601260793_1_cubs-wrigley-field-cookie-lavagetto.

Billy Herman Sidebar:

http://www.bleedcubbieblue.com/2007/2/9/10822/41486.

http://www.baseball-almanac.com/players/player.php?p=hermabi01.

http://www.baseball-reference.com/players/h/hermabi01.shtml.

http://baseballhall.org/hof/herman-billy.

http://www.baseballinwartime.com/player_biographies/herman_billy.htm.

1937: Sammy Slings Redskins to NFL Crown:

Boss, David. The First 50 Years: The Story of the National Football League 1920–1969. New York: Simon and Schuster, 1969 (pgs. 164–5).

http://www.redskins.com/news-and-events/article-1/Flashback-Redskins-First-Season-In-DC/F2F71A18-1B76-4F81-B206-D4D0491DCF6E.

http://www.youtube.com/watch?v=hayDcmtBv7A (newsreel of the game).

http://www.profootballhof.com/hof/member.aspx?PlayerId=21&tab=Capsule.

http://www.pro-football-reference.com/years/1937/leaders.htm.

1938 World Series: Roamin' in the Gloamin' One for the Ages:

Excerpted with permission from: McGrath, Dan and Bob Vanderberg. *162–0: Imagine a Cubs Perfect Season*. Chicago: Triumph Books, 2011.

Rogers Hornsby Sidebar:

http://www.justonebadcentury.com/chicago_cubs_tales_09_32.asp.

http://www.baseball-reference.com/players/h/hornsro01.shtml.

http://www.baseball-almanac.com/players/player.php?p=hornsro01.

1941: With National Eyes Elsewhere, Bears Defend Title:

http://www.pro-football-reference.com/boxscores/194112210chi.htm.

http://www.profootballhof.com/history/2011/1/19/black-and-blue-in-41—-page-2/.

http://books.google.com/books/about/1941_Nfl_Championship_Game.
html?id=QLx1MAEACAAJ.

http://www.youtube.com/watch?v=ny95QZm4mRQ (game highlights).

http://www.history.com/topics/pearl-harbor.

1943: A Heaping Dose of Bad "Luck" for Redskins:

http://bleacherreport.com/articles/357519-one-for-the-ages-sid-luckmans-1943-nfl-
championship-game.

http://www.pro-football-reference.com/boxscores/194312260chi.htm.

http://www.pro-football-reference.com/teams/chi/1943.htm.

http://www.profootballhof.com/hof/member.aspx?PLAYER_ID=135.

http://news.google.com/newspapers?id=mF8aAAAAIBAJ&sjid=
CCMEAAAAIBAJ&pg=4687%2C4437626 (*Milwaukee Journal* game story).

PART IV:
1947: AL Prevails in All-Star Nail-Biter:

http://www.lib.niu.edu/2001/ihy011220.html.

http://www.baseball-reference.com/allstar/.

http://www.baseball-reference.com/boxes/NLS/NLS194707080.shtml.

http://mlb.mlb.com/mlb/history/mlb_asgrecaps_story_headline.jsp?story_
page=recap_1947.

http://www.baseball-almanac.com/asgbox/yr1947as.shtml.

1950: From "Oh No" to "No-No," Jones Tosses Gem:

http://www.baseball-reference.com/players/j/jonessa02.shtml.

http://sportsillustrated.cnn.com/vault/article/magazine/MAG1071140/5/index.htm.

http://www.agonyandivy.com/2011/01/greatest-moments-no-13-sam-jones-no-hitter.
php.

http://books.google.com/books?id=c7EDAAAAMBAJ&pg=PA52&lpg=
PA52&dq=Sam+Jones+no-hitter&source=bl&ots=PN3sUotjkj&sig=
WWxPWBIUFsa3Em2g_yGv2PEuPQQ&hl=en&sa=X&ei=cIYqUb_
WDejXiAKeuYD4Cw&ved=0CFQQ6AEwBDge#v=onepage&q=Sam%20
Jones%20no-hitter&f=false.

http://www.baseball-reference.com/boxes/CHN/CHN195505120.shtml.

http://www.thepostgame.com/blog/throwback/201103/hank-aaron-recalls-toothpick-
sam-jones.

http://chicago.cubs.mlb.com/chc/history/timeline07.jsp.

http://www.examiner.com/article/edwin-jackson-s-no-hitter-shows-similarities-to-
that-of-toothpick-sam-jones-55-years-earlier.

http://www.baseball-almanac.com/boxscore/sam_jones_no_hitter.shtml.

Ernie Banks Sidebar:

Excerpted with Permission from: Vorwald, Bob and Stephen Green. *Cubs Forever:
Memories from the Men Who Lived Them*. Chicago: Triumph Books, 2008.

1958: Stan the Man Joins 3,000-Hit Club:

http://espn.go.com/classic/s/moment010513musial3000.html.

http://baseballhall.org/hof/musial-stan.

http://mlb.mlb.com/video/play.jsp?content_id=25568137&topic_id=40773316&c_
id=mlb.

http://www.stltoday.com/sports/baseball/professional/stan-musial-joins-the—hit-
club/article_e88fe56c-aeaa-5873-9390-6fcf22346434.html.

http://baseballhall.org/media/photo-gallery/stan-musials-3000th-hit.

1960: The New Kid in Town:

http://sports.espn.go.com/mlb/news/story?id=3196704.

http://www.chicagotribune.com/chi-chicagolive-1960-cubs-don-cardwell-no-hitter-video,0,7110473.htmlstory.

http://www.baseball-reference.com/teams/CHC/1960.shtml.

http://www.baseball-almanac.com/teamstats/roster.php?y=1960&t=CHN.

http://articles.chicagotribune.com/1996-07-23/sports/9607230071_1_no-hitter-cubs-moose.

http://www.baseball-reference.com/boxes/CHN/CHN196005152.shtml.

1963: Chicago Defense "Bears" Down:

http://www.chicagotribune.com/news/politics/chi-chicagodays-1963nfl-story,0,2181510.story.

http://www.profootballresearchers.org/Articles/1963_NFL_Championship.pdf.

http://www.youtube.com/watch?v=sUrDH94rYKA (game highlights).

http://www.cogsci.indiana.edu/farg/rehling/bears/1963.html.

http://www.pro-football-reference.com/boxscores/196312290chi.htm.

1965: Rookie Sayers Cuts Through Mud for Record Six TDs:

http://www.chicagonow.com/chicago-tough/2011/08/youtube-clip-of-the-week-sayers-scores-6-touchdowns-bears-61-niners-20/.

http://www.pro-football-reference.com/boxscores/196512120chi.htm.

http://www.history.com/this-day-in-history/nfl-rookie-gale-sayers-ties-single-game-td-record.

http://espn.go.com/sportscentury/features/00016460.html.

http://www.profootballresearchers.org/Coffin_Corner/02-09-043.pdf.

http://www.bearshistory.com/lore/galesayers.aspx.

April 8, 1969: Willie Smith's Opening Day Heroics:

Excerpted with permission from: McGrath, Dan and Bob Vanderberg. *162–0: Imagine a Cubs Perfect Season*. Chicago: Triumph Books, 2011.

Billy Williams Sidebar:

Excerpted with Permission from: Vorwald, Bob and Stephen Green. *Cubs Forever: Memories from the Men Who Lived Them*. Chicago: Triumph Books, 2008.

June 29, 1969: Billy Williams Day:

Excerpted with permission from: McGrath, Dan and Bob Vanderberg. *162–0: Imagine a Cubs Perfect Season*. Chicago: Triumph Books, 2011.

Ron Santo Sidebar:

Excerpted with Permission from: Vorwald, Bob and Stephen Green. *Cubs Forever: Memories from the Men Who Lived Them*. Chicago: Triumph Books, 2008.

August 19, 1969: Lucky Kenny Holtzman and his (First) No-Hitter:

Excerpted with permission from: McGrath, Dan and Bob Vanderberg. *162–0: Imagine a Cubs Perfect Season*. Chicago: Triumph Books, 2011.

Ferguson "Fergie" Jenkins Sidebar:

http://www.baseball-reference.com/players/j/jenkife01.shtml.
http://baseballhall.org/hof/jenkins-ferguson.
http://www.fergiejenkinsfoundation.org/site_fergie.htm.

May 17, 1970: Ernie Belts No. 500:

Excerpted with permission from: McGrath, Dan and Bob Vanderberg. *162–0: Imagine a Cubs Perfect Season*. Chicago: Triumph Books, 2011.

AND

Excerpted with Permission from: Vorwald, Bob and Stephen Green. *Cubs Forever: Memories from the Men Who Lived Them*. Chicago: Triumph Books, 2008.

September 2, 1972: Almost Perfect—Milt Pappas' "Disappointing No-Hitter":

Excerpted with Permission from: Vorwald, Bob and Stephen Green. *Cubs Forever: Memories from the Men Who Lived Them*. Chicago: Triumph Books, 2008.

Part V:
1982: Harry Caray Starts a Singing Tradition:
http://www.harrycarays.com/harry_caray.html
Sandomir, Richard. "Harry Caray, 78, Colorful Baseball Aonnouncer, Dies." *New York Times*, Ferbuary 19, 1998.
Sherman, Ed. "He Took Us Out to the Ballgame." *Chicago Tribune*, February 19, 1998, p. 1. (Available online at: http://articles.chicagotribune.com/1998-02-19/news/9802190134_1_harry-caray-fun-fans).
Yellon, Al. "The Wrigley Seventh-Inning Tradition Is Changing." http://www.bleedcubbieblue.com/2013/2/19/4005844/cubs-seventh-inning-stretch-singers-wrigley-changing.

August 18, 1982: Turning 21 at Wrigley:
LeeElia.com. "The Complete April 29, 1983 Lee Elia Press Conference Tirade." http://www.leeelia.com/elia_tirade.html.
Myers, Doug. *Essential Cubs*. New York: Contemporary Books, 1999 (pg. 344).
Snyder, John. *Cubs Journal*. Cincinnati: Emmis Books, 2005 (pg. 540).

1984: Second City Pandemonium, Orwellian Climax:
Associated Press. "Padres Sign Garvey." *Tuscaloosa News*, December 22, 1982.
Myers, Doug. *Essential Cubs*. New York: Contemporary Books, 1999 (passim).
Orwell, George. *1984*. New York: Signet Classic, 1950.
Shea, Stu. *Wrigley Field: The Unauthorized Biography*. Washington, DC: Brassey's, Inc., 2004.
Stout, Glenn and Richard A. Johnson. *The Cubs: The Complete History of Chicago Cubs Baseball*. Boston: Houghton Mifflin, 2007 (pgs. 324–47).
Yellon, Al. "A Game from Cubs History: September 30, 1984." http://www.bleedcubbieblue.com/2013/1/27/3899522/cubs-history-game-september-30-1984.

Dennis Eckersley Sidebar:

Wancho, Joseph. "Dennis Eckersley." SABR Baseball Biography Project. http://sabr. org/bioproj/person/98aaf620

Wulf, Steve. "The Paintmaster." Sports Illustrated, August 24, 1992, 62–73.

Ryne Sandberg Sidebar:

Excerpted with Permission from: Vorwald, Bob and Stephen Green. *Cubs Forever: Memories from the Men Who Lived Them*. Chicago: Triumph Books, 2008.

June 23, 1984: The Sandberg Game:

Excerpted with permission from: McGrath, Dan and Bob Vanderberg. *162–0: Imagine a Cubs Perfect Season*. Chicago: Triumph Books, 2011.

Andre Dawson Sidebar:

D'Addona, Dan. "Andre Dawson." SABR Baseball Biography Project. SABR.org. http://sabr.org/bioproj/person/8ce7c5bf.

Philadelphia Inquirer Wire Services. "Andre Dawson Signs a Two-Year Contract with Cubs." http://articles.philly.com/1988-03-29/sports/26279846_1_fill-in-the-blank-contract-collusion-case-first-female-umpire.

Rigolsby, Tracy. "Dawson Induction a Rare Expos Moment." http://msn.foxsports. com/mlb/story/Hall-of-fame-enshrinee-andre-dawson-casts-rare-spotlight-on-montreal-expos-072410.

August 8, 1988: Let There Be Lights!:

Excerpted with Permission from: Vorwald, Bob and Stephen Green. *Cubs Forever: Memories from the Men Who Lived Them*. Chicago: Triumph Books, 2008.

1989: Zim's 89er Rush:

Shea, Stu. *Wrigley Field: The Unauthorized Biography*. Washington, DC: Brassey's, Inc., 2004.

Snyder, John. *Cubs Journal*. Cincinnati: Emmis Books, 2005 (pgs. 577–83).

Stout, Glenn and Richard A. Johnson. *The Cubs: The Complete History of Chicago Cubs Baseball*. Boston: Houghton Mifflin, 2007 (pgs. 345–73).

1990: All-Star Charm, Just Not Lucky:

Baseball Almanac. "1990 All-Star Game." http://www.baseball-almanac.com/asgbox/yr1990as.shtml.

MLB.com. "Home Run Derby History." http://mlb.mlb.com/mlb/history/hr_derby.jsp

Shea, Stu. *Wrigley Field: The Unauthorized Biography*. Washington, DC: Brassey's, Inc., 2004 (pgs. 308–9).

Mark Grace Sidebar:

http://www.markgrace.com/bio_cubs.html.

http://www.baseball-reference.com/players/g/gracema01.shtml.

http://www.bleedcubbieblue.com/2013/1/31/3937572/mark-grace-guilty-dui-scottsdale-arizona; http://kjzz.org/content/1301/mark-grace-takes-plea-will-work-dbacks-again.

1998: The Season of Thrills:

Excerpted with Permission from: Vorwald, Bob and Stephen Green. *Cubs Forever: Memories from the Men Who Lived Them*. Chicago: Triumph Books, 2008.

Sammy Sosa Sidebar:

http://espn.go.com/chicago/mlb/story/_/id/8873871/sammy-sosa-says-chicago-cubs-jersey-retired.

http://www.baseball-reference.com/players/s/sosasa01.shtm.

http://www.sammysosa.info/biography/.

http://www.biography.com/people/sammy-sosa-189155.

http://www.latinosportslegends.com/sosa.htm.

http://chicagoist.com/2013/01/09/baseball_hall_of_fame_shuts_out_bon.php.

Part VI:

2003: From Bounty to Bartman:

http://www.goatriders.org/cubs-101/in-dusty-we-trusty.

http://www.baseball-reference.com/boxes/CHN/CHN200310140.shtml.

http://www.baseball-reference.com/leagues/NL/2003-fielding-leaders.shtml.

http://articles.chicagotribune.com/2011-09-26/sports/ct-spt-0927-bartman-
chicago—20110927_1_cubs-five-outs-scapegoat-bartman-alex-gibney.

Carlos Zambrano Sidebar:

http://bleacherreport.com/articles/1445544-5-mlb-free-agents-you-dont-want-near-
your-teams-clubhouse/page/4.

http://www.bleedcubbieblue.com/2013/2/14/3989158/carlos-zambrano-japan-rumor-
cubs-marlins-news.

http://www.baseball-reference.com/players/z/zambrca01.shtml.

2005: Greg Maddux's 3000th Strikeout:

Excerpted with Permission from: Vorwald, Bob and Stephen Green. *Cubs Forever:
Memories from the Men Who Lived Them*. Chicago: Triumph Books, 2008.

2007 Season: From Embers to Flames:

http://scores.espn.go.com/mlb/recap?gameId=271006116.

http://scores.espn.go.com/mlb/recap?gameId=271004129.

http://scores.espn.go.com/mlb/recap?gameId=271003129.

http://www.baseball-reference.com/teams/ARI/2007.shtml.

http://www.goatriders.org/cubs-101/2007-cubs.

http://sports.espn.go.com/mlb/recap?gameId=270601116.

http://sports.espn.go.com/mlb/news/story?id=2910079.

http://www.baseball-reference.com/teams/CHC/2007.shtml.

http://www.chicago-cubs-fan.com/2007-Chicago-Cubs.html.

Alfonso Soriano Sidebar:

http://sports.yahoo.com/mlb/players/615.

http://chicago.cubs.mlb.com/team/player.jsp?player
id=150093#gameType='S'&sectionType=career&statType=
1&season=2013&level='ALL'.

http://www.jockbio.com/Bios/Soriano/Soriano_bio.html.

http://www.searchnetworth.com/alfonso-soriano-net-worth/.

http://baseball.about.com/od/profiles/p/soriano.htm.

2008 Season: A Tragic Centennial:

http://scores.espn.go.com/mlb/recap?gameId=281004119.

http://bleacherreport.com/articles/88872-chicago-cubs-2008-season-in-brief-review.

http://www.baseball-reference.com/teams/CHC/2008.shtml.

http://www.baseball-reference.com/leagues/NL/2008-standard-pitching.shtml.

The Cry That Never Dies: "Wait 'Til Next Year!":

http://www.baseball-reference.com/teams/CHC/2012.shtml.

http://www.baseball-reference.com/teams/CHC/2011.shtml.

http://www.baseball-reference.com/teams/CHC/2010.shtml.

http://www.baseball-reference.com/teams/CHC/2009.shtml.

http://espn.go.com/chicago/mlb/story/_/id/8957035/chicago-cubs-chairman-tom-
ricketts-happy-progress-made-theo-epstein.

http://nbcsports.msnbc.com/id/51282651/ns/sports-baseball/.

http://www.usatoday.com/story/sports/mlb/2013/01/12/theo-epstein-no-more-lovable-
losers-for-cubs/1828683/.

Acknowledgments

I am very grateful to have the privilege of working with some very talented and knowledgeable baseball writers including: Bill Chastain, Eric Short, Matthew Silverman, Marty Strasen, and Sue Sveum. My publisher arranged usage of some additional and wonderful material, which are various excerpts from several other authors of Triumph Books: Bob Vorwald (*Cubs Forever*, 2008), and coauthors Dan McGrath and Bob Vanderberg (*162–0: Imagine a Cubs Perfect Season*, 2011).

I was honored to have this book published by Triumph Books. This is my third title with them, and I am very grateful to president Mitch Rogatz for taking on this title and the help of Triumph's Noah Amstadter in bringing it in. The advice and hard work of several key men at Triumph added greatly to the quality of my text and I am therefore indebted to my editor, Adam Motin, and his colleague Laine Morreau, the latter who helped immeasurably with the acquisition of photos. And thank you, Curt Matthews, head of IPG, who steered this title toward Triumph.

The accompanying DVD documentary was edited by Jack Piantino, whose fine work and friendship I've enjoyed for more than 10 years now, through 15 documentaries that he has helped me produce. The one that accompanies this book is among the finest we have ever produced. Thanks, Jack!

I could not have found better show hosts for my DVD documentary than my longtime friend Lou Boudreau Jr., who recruited his friend (and now my friend too) Ron Santo Jr.; and Jim Boudreau too, who participated in the taping. All of us were elated that WGN's Jeff Hill invited us to their studios to record the voice over, which benefited from the professionalism of his staff which includes Kristin Decker, Jim Holland, Alex Quigley, and Bill White.

Thank you!
Les Krantz

Photo Credits